To:

— Ralph Weiss —

my best to you, and
Associated Volume Buyers

Barry Osmin

WHEN RIDING A DEAD HORSE, FOR HEAVENS SAKE...
DISMOUNT!

Barry Asmus

AMERIPRESS
Phoenix, Arizona
1-800-225-3864

Library of Congress Catalog Card Number: 94-74514

ISBN: 0-9640421-3-4 (Cloth)
ISBN: 0-9640421-4-2 (Paper)

Cover design: James Cowlin and Mike Slominski

Published in the United States by
AmeriPress
3420 East Shea Blvd., Suite 235
Phoenix, Arizona 85028

Manufactured in the United States of America

10 9 8 7 6 5 4 3 2

To my friend Jerry Hill.

CONTENTS

PREFACE

Imagine the surprise of the old cowboy as he sat on his once sick but now dead horse. "Dang it," he said. "This has never happened before." Neither has what you are about to read.

Dismount! is about the expiration of the familiar but dying steeds of the Industrial Age. Big government doesn't work. Neither do hierarchical corporations, government schools, or grand health care schemes. The swayback policies of Clinton and clones are wheezing and about to collapse.

Centralism was always dubious. It is now a dead horse. The political systems and economic doctrines of intervention that evolved through the Agricultural and Industrial Ages are no longer relevant in an age of empowerment.

Talk radio, Internet, fax machines, telecomputers, CNN, and C-SPAN are just the first shots of an Information Revolution that will completely transform the way we work and govern ourselves. People informed are people empowered. Microelectronics and digital technologies are pulling decision making downward and outward from central authorities of all kinds. Decentralization of information always leads to a decentralization of power.

Enlightened self interest is a natural phenomenon. The market is. Gravity is. Capitalism happens and will keep on happening. Private property, limited government, voluntary exchange, free markets and economic growth are time tested ideas that work.

The triumph of the individual is at hand. When riding a dead horse, for heavens sake . . . Dismount!

PART I

WHAT IN THE WORLD IS GOING ON?

Chapter One

INTRODUCTION

The scene: The American Bankers' annual meeting in Honolulu, November 10, 1981. In the audience are 2500 bank presidents, the who's who of American banking. They are dressed to the nines—expensive suits, fifty-dollar ties. They are there to hear Alan Greenspan, later to be chairman of the powerful Federal Reserve Board, previously a top economic advisor to President Gerald Ford and now an advisor to Ronald Reagan.

Every place setting has three forks, two wine glasses, big flared napkins and beautifully sculpted pineapples. The ballroom is breathtaking.

The master of ceremonies comes to the podium. The room goes silent.

"Ladies and gentlemen," he says, "we have some bad news and some good news. The bad news is that Alan Greenspan is in the hospital. We are sorry and we wish him a speedy recovery. The good news is that today, just in from Idaho, we have an associate professor of economics from Boise State University, Barry Asmus."

Up to the podium walks a young man in a light-blue leisure suit. His tie is the best that five dollars can buy at

J.C. Penney's. He has been wearing his ten dollar shirt for twenty hours straight.

Who is this guy?

Me. That's right. I'm Barry Asmus.

I begin my speech, haltingly. I'm scared to death. It's one thing to teach eighteen-year old kids just off the Idaho potato farms. It's another thing to talk to the upper crust of American banking. What can I tell them?

Actually, a lot.

I tell these pillars of capitalism that free markets, limited government and voluntary exchange have been the most liberating ideas ever in mankind's history. I tell them how freedom has allowed ordinary people to do extraordinary things—the oil wells in Texas, the Sears Tower in Chicago, Disneyland in southern California. I tell them that if you were to make a list of all the things that capitalism produces and provides, you would fill a library. But now, I tell them, we have moved a long way from freedom. Now, government takes almost half of our income and tells us what to do with the other half.

How, I ask, did this happen? I tell them of my farmer friends in eastern Colorado, who believe in freedom and even fought for it in World War II. They are willing to wave the flag of free enterprise with their right hand, but accept government farm subsidies with their left. With their right hands raised, they say, "I'm for capitalism, but . . ." With their left hands held out, they say they need government help. They are not alone. Everyone says they are for free enterprise, but . . . Chrysler is all for free enterprise, but not if Americans want to buy from Japan and not if Chrysler could go bankrupt. Small business owners are all for capitalism, but many insist on federal subsidies. And bankers believe in free markets, except when it comes to competition for small depositors.

"I'm for capitalism, but . . ."

"I'm for capitalism, but . . ."

"Ladies and gentlemen," I say, "capitalism is drowning in a sea of buts."

They laugh. They are having a good time. I am relieved.

I speak for forty-five minutes. The bankers—all 2,500 of them—give me a standing ovation. In the next few years, I will speak at bankers' conventions in forty-seven states. A week before this speech, I was a professor of economics at a small university. Now I will be speaking all across the country.

How did this happen?

Over a period of fifteen years, I have given hundreds of free speeches and thousands of university lectures and never once did I think of a career in public speaking. I could not imagine that people would pay money to listen to a professor, especially in economics.

In fact, I was always delighted to be invited to speak. And having taught the principle TANSTAAFL for over a decade, (There Ain't No Such Thing As A Free Lunch), I was finding out there were lots of free lunches. I'd give a speech. They'd buy my lunch. Trade, after all, is about voluntary exchange for mutual benefit. I always felt that I was getting the good deal. Words for food. As the beer ad says, it just doesn't get any better than this.

And then late one afternoon John Palmer, the president of a speakers bureau, called and asked me if I could possibly leave Boise immediately for the bankers speech in Hawaii.

I called my wife to let her know the details, and with nine dollars in my pocket and my worn, light blue leisure suit, no luggage, no toothbrush, no nothing, I was off.

That was the start of a whole new career. I am still in it. I am a professional speaker. My passion is in sharing my knowledge of economics and business with as many people as possible, to encourage them toward individual achievement, and to explain the workings of a free market, limited government system.

I appear on the same stage as British Prime Minister Margaret Thatcher, management guru Tom Peters, and U.N. Ambassador Jeanne Kirkpatrick. I have hobnobbed with Malcolm S. Forbes, Jr., Editor-in-Chief of *Forbes Magazine*, John Fund, editorial page, the *Wall Street Journal*, and Pete duPont, former governor of Delaware. And I have learned a lot.

What you read in this book is what I have distilled from my conversations with these thinkers as well as from the important books I read as an economist. I know how the world works. I know how business works. I know how government works—or doesn't. It is not because I am smart. It is because I listen. I have been around smart people and I have read their books.

Here is what I have learned.

Big government is about to crumble. Signs of its demise are everywhere. Each hour the information economy transfers billions of dollars around the planet, stripping political leaders of control over their economies. The ability of governments to collect taxes, the ultimate foundation of state power, is reduced with every advance of the global economy. As information empowers citizens, top-down social engineering by government is increasingly rejected as an anachronism. The twilight of sovereignty spells the dawn of a new day.

The liberal activist Clinton Administration is out of sync with voters and out of touch with the new reality. On November 8, 1994, liberal Democrats bit the dust. On November 5, 1996, Clinton will do the same. Government! Don't just do something. Stand there!

Big government no longer works. The evidence of this revolution is worldwide. From Japan to Germany, and all places in-between, political solutions are being replaced by free markets.

Government leaders have become impotent. Oblivious to change, they resemble mainframes talking to each other in a PC world. World leaders understand neither globalization nor the triumph of the individual. Politicians think there is a political crisis. In reality, they have ceased to be important.

The Fortune 500 is ending as the monolithic palace structures of corporations give way to the small, the agile, and the quick. The company office will be wherever employees want to live. Hierarchical organizations are being abandoned. Most jobs will eventually be in the home.

Monopolistic government schooling will be replaced by a competitive school system based on parental choice. Competition between goods and services improves quality in the free market; it will do the same for public education.

The mechanistic economic doctrines of interventionists will be superseded by those who understand the economy as a dynamic social organism. Command and control is over. Centralism is dead. The market is. The market happens. The market works.

We are about to enter one of the most pivotal moments of history. The old world is being rapidly displaced, and the future is increasingly ours to create.

There are no more trends, mega or otherwise. Social, political and economic trends require that something stay still long enough to respond. When everything changes at once, trend loses all meaning.

The Information Age is not a trend. It is a revolution that threatens all existing power bases by redistributing control, access and knowledge. When people get information, they want to participate. They do not want government or anyone else making decisions for them. This is a revolution of power flowing to customers, citizens and individuals, and away from governments, corporations and central planners of all types.

Size no longer matters. It is not necessarily the large and the strong who survive but rather those that can adapt to change. Yesterday, it was the big eating the small; today, it is the fast eating the slow.

National institutions are becoming ineffective. Political parties, the media (ABC, CBS, NBC, the New York Times), big labor unions and even big cities will experience ongoing erosions of power. Massive disintermediation is wide-spread as shoppers by-pass the old infrastructure and gravitate toward home shopping.

Entrepreneurship is about creative destruction. This book is about a radical economic and political transformation rooted in information and globalization that will make entrepreneurs and individuals as powerful as Kings and Queens of times past.

Chapter Two

INFORMATION HAS
CONSEQUENCES

The year? 1840. You are a farmer and have taken a break one Saturday afternoon to watch a demonstration by a new guy in town. His name is Cyrus McCormick. His invention? The McCormick Reaper. "How much reaping can your reaper reap?" you ask. His answer: "My machine can do the work of 15 men."

McCormick's mechanical reaper was probably the most significant single invention of American farming between 1800 and 1860. Replacing human labor with machinery expedited the harvesting process thereby saving crops formerly lost to weather.

Nevertheless, you look at your fellow farmers in disbelief: "Where will we all work if this contraption catches on? Looks to me like we'll all be unemployed."

And catch on it did. Thousands of machines were manufactured and sold. In addition to the reaper were plows, tractors, planters, disks, harrows, combines, fertilizers and hybrid seeds which caused the number of farmers to fall from 50 percent of the population in 1850 to less than 3 percent in 1994. Even so, American farmers today still feed everybody in America and export about $40 billion of agricultural product besides.

Where did they all go? What did they all do? Would machines destroy jobs?

The year? 1900. The setting is at a meeting of the American Candle-Makers Association. Candle making has had a long history and is a skill that has employed tens of thousands of people over the centuries. Thomas Alva Edison is one of the speakers.

You have just watched this inventor with a strange middle name demonstrate a light bulb. What if people like his idea? What will happen to all the candle makers? After all, candles are the main source of indoor lighting. The more you think about what you hear the less you like about what you see.

Yes, there will be some who will praise Edison and get excited about his invention. You even overhear one lady say "Why Tom, without your light bulb we'd all be watching television by candle light."

But, those with clearer heads see the damage tinkerers like Tom will cause. The editor of the town newspaper, in fact, sides with the candle industry. He runs a front page article titled, "TRAGEDY STRIKES THE CANDLE INDUSTRY."

Question: Did the candle makers find new jobs?

The year? 1910. You are a member of the American Buggy Whip Association, and the 250th annual convention is about to conclude.

The last speaker, you are told, will be brief. His name is Henry Ford. This U.S. automotive pioneer invented mass production and the assembly line. His first car was built in a barn at the turn of the century. In 1903, he founded the Ford Motor Company and in 1908 made famous his Model T, black only, four cylinder engine car. After Ford finishes explaining his T, you still have a nagging question: "Henry, if everybody buys one of those (pointing to the car) where will they use one of these (making the motion of using a buggy whip)?"

Ford's answer is brief. "They won't."

You look at your friends in disbelief. "What about whips? What about horses? What about buggies? What about hay raisers?"

Even economists agree that the horseless carriage will cause massive unemployment. Think about it. The average horse poops forty-five pounds a day. Assuming one horse for every four people, a city of one million people will produce 11,250,000 pounds of horse poop a day. Assuming a good pooper scooper can scoop a ton a day, the city will have to employ about 5,600 people to clean its streets. Unemployment among buggy whip makers, horse raisers and pooper scoopers would be staggering if the horseless carriage carried the day.

Question: Did all the buggy whip makers find work?

The reaper, the light bulb, the automobile and subsequent inventions, caused a massive shift in the way people worked, where they lived and how they lived. The Agricultural Age gave way to the Industrial Age. Life changed forever.

The tidal waves presented in this chapter and discussed in this book are about that kind of revolutionary change, and more. This time, however, the driver of change will involve a different kind of machine. Advanced technology and the personal computer will transform society in ways the reaper, the light bulb and the automobile could not. The political systems, social structures and economic doctrines that have served mankind for hundreds of years, for good or for ill, will be toppled. Few institutions will be able to stand the force of the incoming tide.

We are witnessing a revolution like no other.
It will change the way the world works.
Every human being will feel the ripple.

Big government will be beaten down. Hierarchical business structures will fall. Central authorities, central power plants and central almost everything will be washed away. Politics will devolve. Free markets and the contract society will rise.

We are witnessing a revolution like no other. It will change the way the world works. Every human being will feel the ripple.

Greatness no longer belongs to empires. It has gravitated to individuals. While the big story of the 1980s was globalization and the competitiveness of business, the hallmark of the 1990s will be the collapse of hierarchy and the triumph of the individual. Large hierarchical corporations are being undermined by decentralized, responsive, consumer-oriented companies.

Hordes of people everywhere are demanding that government bug out of their lives; that state control be drastically reduced. Government's iron grip on monopolistic educational institutions will first crack and then be absorbed by choice and competition. The command and control economic doctrines that have served mankind so poorly will also be discarded as antiquated relics. Historical forces are propelling a worldwide trend toward free-market economies and away from planners, politicians and power structures that have made life so disagreeable.

Freedom is breaking out like a rash. It is a virus for which there is no antidote. The triumph of the individual is at hand. Information has consequences. Here are two main ones.

INFORMATION EMPOWERS PEOPLE

Today, almost everybody has access to voluminous amounts of information. Individuals are being empowered in a way that only kings and generals once enjoyed. They could rule, control, dictate and command us because they were the only ones with access to information. That day is over.

Microelectronics is pulling decision making downward and outward from central authorities of all kinds. A decentralization of information inevitably leads to a decentralization of power. Top down decision making no longer works. Command technologies of control are being preempted by the technologies of freedom. Even Castro must know the Party is over. Soon, Clinton will too.

Central governments throughout the world are quaking
in their boots. Why? Because they are becoming
irrelevant. Big government will collapse for the same
reason as the Berlin Wall: INFORMATION. As Harry
Truman said, "Put a Sears, Roebuck and Company catalog
in every communist home on Friday, and by Monday
morning, communism will be finished."

People informed are people empowered. Armed with
information and knowledge, they simply do not want other
people making decisions for them. In particular, they do
not want government deciding what they can decide for
themselves.

MATTER DOESN'T MATTER MUCH ANYMORE

A second consequence of the Information Age is the
increasing importance of knowledge in the production of
wealth. The new source of wealth is not material. It is
information. The value of a video cassette is not the tape.
It is the information in the movie. The value is in content,
not the package. A book might cost only a few dollars to
print. The rest of the twenty dollars goes to the author,
publisher and distributor. Knowledge applied to work to
create value is how the world will work.

Information is replacing raw materials. It used to take,
for example, 160 pounds of aluminum to manufacture one
thousand aluminum cans. Today, it takes just thirty
pounds. A silicon chip is 1 percent raw material and 99
percent mental input. U.S. exports in dollar terms have
doubled in the past six years, but the physical weight of
our exports has hardly changed. Twenty years ago a desk
top calculator might have weighed ten pounds. The one

you use now probably weighs less than an ounce and can do considerably more.

Knowledge extraction, integration and application are replacing the shipment of raw materials from remote locations to manufacturing centers as the dominant world business. Knowledge has become the main source of economic value. Matter matters less and less. Knowledge and ideas matter more and more.

Until just a few years ago, telephones consumed most of the world's copper production. But now, copper wire is being replaced almost entirely by fiber optic cable made from glass, made from sand. Copper is a scarce resource. Sand is almost infinite in abundance.

THE ELECTRIC HIGHWAY

Before the end of this decade, a billion switches stacked on a silicon chip the size of your thumbnail will turbo-charge the ongoing personal computer revolution. The advance in technology is determined mainly by our ability to process information. It is doubling every few years. Computers are today's machine of the mind that free us from the drudgery of information processing much like Caterpillars free us from the drudgery of dirt processing.

Labor is highly mobile. What do you need to be in business around the world? Four things: a telephone, a modem, a fax machine, and a brain.

Capital is like quicksilver. Once fixed, capital is now fugitive. It can instantly get up on the electronic highway, go where it is wanted, and stay where it is well treated. As information and knowledge are forged into capital, the world is connected by blips on a computer screen that race across countries and continents in micro seconds. The dollar amounts we are talking about are huge; sometimes one hundred times larger than current world trade flows on an annual basis.

National boundaries are increasingly porous and meaningless as computers, printers, photocopiers, fax machines, telephones and televisions become the new guns of liberty.

Computers are today's machine of the mind that free us from the drudgery of information processing much like Caterpillars free us from the drudgery of dirt processing.

In an economy that is extremely integrated and complicated, no one individual has the ability to understand the intricacies of all the connected relationships. And, therefore, we can be quite confident that central planners can't understand them either. Grand designs by either government or corporate hierarchies are ineffective. Top-down monopolistic structures no longer work.

Today, as never before, economic and political decision making must reside with those closest to the activity, the customer and the citizen. Bureaucracies and hierarchies are becoming overwhelmed because they are not structured to make quick decisions.

Technology is rendering governments impotent. A person with the skills to write a billion dollars worth of software programming is able to walk right by a customs officer with nothing of value to declare. Faced with the prospect of a tax increase or more government regulation, citizens will take themselves to more hospitable climates.

Resources are no longer found just in the ground. They are increasingly in the minds, hearts and spirits of individuals, business people, and inventors throughout the world.

In short, people are tired of being governed, regimented, and controlled. As the information/technological age lubricates markets and drives transaction costs to zero, every function of government will be a candidate for privatization. Hierarchical corporations will be decentralized and employees empowered. Entrepreneurship and the contract society will be the most common form of business. Top-down monopolistic education will give way to individual choice. And the mechanistic economic doctrines that view the economy as a machine will be replaced with those that understand the economy as a spontaneous, living social organism.

Globalization and the triumph of the individual are at hand.

We are moving to what 17th century historian Baruch Spinoza described: "The last end of the state is not to dominate men, nor restrain them by fear; rather it is to set free each man from fear, that he may live and act with full security and without injury to himself or his neighbor . . . the end of the state is really liberty."

Chapter Three

FREEDOM IS THE MAINSPRING OF HUMAN PROGRESS

Henry Grady Weaver wrote a book in 1947 entitled *Freedom is the Mainspring of Human Progress.* It sold almost a million copies, in part, because he was right.

People all over the world risk their lives to get to freedom. More freedom, more bread. More freedom, more income. More freedom, more opportunity. History has proven that when people are given a chance to vote with their feet, they will vote for freedom every time.

Just look at Hong Kong: a city built by waves of people making the dangerous trek from China. They sail in rickety vessels through the South China Sea, suffer asphyxiation in crowded rail cars, and vault high voltage fences to get there. While Mao Tse Tung's China was stuck in a prison house of economic failures, Hong Kong represented opportunity. Millions of mainland Chinese risked their lives in their flight from China. But why come to one of the most densely populated places on the planet and crowd into an inhospitable terrain? Hong Kong is dependent on its neighbors for almost all of its resources, including basics like water. If you think China is populated, you should see Hong Kong. What is the magnet-like force that keeps people coming?

It is now widely understood that in Hong Kong, freedom, free markets and free trade have produced standards of living higher than any in Asia. Unemployment is usually less than 2 percent, and its per capita income has now surpassed that of its colonial protector, Great Britain.

History has proven that when people are given
a chance to vote with their feet, they will vote for
freedom every time.

I know what you're asking. Doesn't the Premier of China allow freedom of speech? The answer is, yes, he does. But, unfortunately, he does not allow freedom after the speech.

Wherever you go, freedom works.

I'll never forget my time at the Berlin Wall prior to its collapse. In West Berlin, I see a city brimming with economic activity. In East Berlin I see a city drowning in economic blight. Look one way, and see a vibrant, exciting city. Yet, go through Checkpoint Charlie into East Berlin, and see a different world: Gray. Drab. Very few goods on the shelves and not many cars on the streets. It is hard to believe that this used to be one city. All Germans, but divided as day is from night. Freedom is clearly the mainspring of human progress.

It was more than just the collapse of a wall in 1989. It was the collapse of an idea. Socialism is finished. Everybody knows it. Even socialists know it doesn't work. With the exception of many American university professors and the folks in the Clinton Administration, most people in the world realize that socialism is a construct that will not work in practice. It was wrong about profits, wrong about private property, and wrong about people. It was wrong about everything. Built on the rotten pillars of public ownership and the labor theory of value, socialism's demise was predicted sixty years ago by the Austrian economists Ludwig von Mises and F. A. Hayek.

Even the American socialist economist and widely influential author Robert Heilbroner, in an article in the quarterly magazine "Dissent" admits it:

> Capitalism has been as unmistakable a success as socialism has been a failure. But here is the part that is hard to swallow. It has been the Friedmans, Hayeks, von Mises who have maintained that capitalism would flourish and that socialism would develop incurable ailments. All three have regarded capitalism as the "natural" system of free men; all have maintained that left to its own devices capitalism would achieve material growth more successfully than any other system. From this admittedly impressionistic and incomplete sampling I draw the following discomforting generalization: The farther to the right one looks, the more prescient has been the historical foresight; the farther to the left, the less so.

Just as Mises's and Hayek's scholarly work showed, it was information that brought both socialism and the Berlin Wall down. Revolutions do not occur until people learn that there is an alternative to their way of life. Information empowers people. Government can no longer fool people, because power is moving to the people.

The new electronic infrastructure turns the whole planet on to the cause of freedom. Free-market capitalism has shown again and again that it will win against any competing form of political and economic arrangement.

Technology has replaced tanks. The seventy-year iron reign of the communists proved that they could control tanks but that they could not control fax machines. The Technological Revolution produced an Information Age in which the totalitarian control of information so necessary to a socialist government was rendered futile.

One year after the Persian Gulf War, I had lunch with CNN's John Holliman and the Nebraska Bankers Association. He told the following story.

As you might remember, John, Peter Arnett, and Bernard Shaw were broadcasting events live as they happened. It was two o'clock in the morning, January 17, 1991. CNN was the only network carrying the story because the other major networks had lost their satellite hookups. It was a night that will be hard to forget.

On the afternoon of the first day of the war, a friend of John's called him at the hotel and asked him if he would like to drive around the city of Baghdad to witness the night's destruction. Of course, John agreed. As they were driving down one of the major streets, a Tomahawk Cruise Missile flew to their intersection, made a gradual right turn, headed down the boulevard and slammed into the Presidential Palace. The place was blown to smithereens. All John's friend could say was, "Damn."

As they continued their drive through the city, John noticed a ten story telephone building that had a large corner section of the 8th floor blown away. He asked his friend what was on the 8th floor? The reply, "That's where the computers were."

Upon returning to the hotel, John, Peter and Bernie were informed that CNN was being kicked out of Baghdad. Arnett did get to stay but John, Bernard and the rest of the CNN crew were forced to leave.

The next evening, John and the crew loaded their cars and took off for Jordan. As they made their way along the 160 mile highway, with runway lights on both sides, John noticed scud missiles underneath each overpass. There were dozens. When they arrived in Jordan, John could hardly wait to call the Pentagon and tell them what he had seen.

"This is John Holliman with CNN. Give me someone high ranking, and hurry please," an out-of-breath Holliman pleaded. And who finally answered his call? General Colin Powell.

"General Powell. This is John Holliman from CNN in Jordan. Sir, on our trip from Baghdad we saw dozens of scud missiles hidden beneath the highway overpasses and we thought you would like to know."

John's heart was pounding and his adrenaline was raging like a river.

General Powell responded, "John, settle down. You left Baghdad at 1700 hours, correct?"

John replied, "Yes, we did"

"Your crew was in three cars, the third car was blue, and you were driving it, is that right?" the General said.

"Yes Sir," Holliman replied.

"John, at about 70 kilometers you stopped alongside the road and got out to go to the bathroom," the General laughed.

"Yes, sir. Yes, sir. But how did . . ."

Powell boomed out. "John, we were watching. We've been waiting for you to get off the highway."

Satellites, computers, cellular phones, fax machines and other technological marvels have changed the way we do everything, including how we fight our wars. Technology is now more important than tanks. After all, we only had twenty Stealth Bombers in the Gulf—an airplane so jam-packed with technology that massive numbers weren't necessary. Brute strength means less and less. Victory goes to the smart.

Fortunately, the cornerstone of freedom is not war. If Hitler would have won, there would be no freedom. Castro's control has not brought freedom, nor have the cold war communists in either the Soviet Union or Red China. So what is it? If the wealth of a nation is its people, and if freedom really is the mainspring of human progress, then what is the prerequisite to freedom?

The answer is private property. Economists have long known that the institutions of capitalism, common law, a court system to adjudicate disputes, and property rights have evolved along with open exchange in the marketplace.

Nobody summarized the idea better than Daniel Webster: "Liberty and property. One and inseparable. Now and forever."

Gerald Scully, in his book *Statism versus Individualism and Economic Progress in Latin America,* shows the relationship between freedom, property rights and economic progress. Free societies allow individuals to engage in mutually beneficial exchange and take full advantage of opportunities for specialization and trade. Most of the world has come to understand these important ideas.

Nobody summarized the idea better than Daniel Webster: "Liberty and property. One and inseparable. Now and forever."

Yes, democracy is better than anointing a king. But deciding how the rulers are chosen is not as important as the rules they enact. Rules determine outcomes. Free markets, open trade, stable property rights, and the rule of law lead to prosperity. Democracy is about politics and redistribution. Most democracies begin with limited government and unlimited opportunities. But they inevitably gravitate toward unlimited government and limited opportunities.

Margaret Thatcher tried to reverse this trend by weaning the British economy away from public ownership. Her policies of privatization moved one-third of the government work force into the private sector, caused two million housing units to be privatized and forced hundreds of firms like British Telecom, Jaguar, British Airways and British Steel to be uncoupled from government management.

Thus began what the Wall Street Journal called the "Sale of the Century"—one of the largest global transfers of property in modern history: from Buenos Aires to

Budapest, from Washington to Auckland; from steel mills to delicatessens, privatization has become the new economic mantra. Has it worked? Yes.

Privatization is a fairly new concept. The word "privatize" did not appear in Webster's New Collegiate Dictionary until 1983. Since then, privatization in new and emerging markets has surged. Roughly 2,700 state-owned enterprises were transferred to private hands in over ninety-five countries from 1988 to 1995. Revenues generated were approximately $275 billion. Japan has produced the largest privatization deal to date with its $22.8 billion sell-off of Nippon Telegraph and Telephone. The planned privatization of Germany's Deutsche Telekom in early 1996 is even bigger—totaling $45 billion.

"Margaret Thatcher privatized three or four firms a year," said Prime Minister Vaclac Klaus, chief architect of the Czech Republic's lightning privatization campaign. "We have been privatizing twice that figure per day."

All of Europe is now privatizing.

Latin and South America are also marching toward stabilized property rights and the market.

Even under a dictatorship, Chile managed to keep all of its privatization efforts of the last two decades in place. Columbia has instituted massive privatization programs, even to the extent of privatizing their social security program. In Mexico, President Salinas seemed determined to follow suit.

Most countries have come to realize what it takes to produce wealth. President Salinas is just one example of what is happening around the world. In 1987, he asked why Mexicans live so poorly? Just look at the contrast between Tiajuana and San Diego. How could a few miles produce such radically different lifestyles?

Is it because Mexicans are lazy? No, they are hard-working. Well, then, what is the problem?

Salinas concluded there were several problems inhibiting the Mexican economy.

First, marginal tax rates were too high. He lowered them from 68 percent to 35 percent. Taxes matter. Incentives matter. People's decisions to work, save, invest and exercise entrepreneurship depend to a large degree on whether taxes are high or low.

Second, Salinas worked hard to make sure that the free trade agreement with the United States would pass. Unlike Ross Perot, who believes trade is about warfare, Salinas believes that trade is about win/win. Hopefully, he will be able to convince the "little hand grenade with a bad haircut" from Texas that trade is about mutual gains from voluntary exchange and that it will benefit both countries. Mr. Buchanan, are you listening?

Then, President Salinas made his big move. He stabilized property rights. He was disgusted with the fact that whenever people succeed in Mexico, the government intervenes and nationalizes their property. Without stable property rights, there are no incentives to produce. Government must get out of the business of business. President Salinas has already privatized over 1,400 government owned firms. His successor, Ernesto Zedillo, agrees. And though his devaluation of the Peso was a terrible mistake, ninety million Mexicans are working their way to middle-class prosperity.

But economic miracles are not just occurring in Mexico. Look at Chile. Chile is privatizing everything, including its social security system. Travel to Santiago if you want to see another miraculous economic transformation.

Argentina is also experiencing an economic lift off. Argentina should have been another United States 90 years ago. But without property rights, incentives were non-existent. Whenever people succeeded, government would confiscate their property. All that is changing as Argentina privatizes, deregulates, and lowers taxes.

India is another example of privatizing and following a more capitalist course. In fact, about half of the world's population is now on a path of very high growth and industrialization, as opposed to 10 percent just after World War II. Privatization and free markets always produce growth. Countries that move toward freedom achieve prosperity as well.

Even communist countries are privatizing.

Private property is the prerequisite for freedom, and freedom is the mainspring of human progress. If you don't believe that, let me ask you a question: When was the last time that you washed a rental car?

Is Deng Xiaoping, a communist? Yes. Would he take your head off at Tiananmen Square? In a second. But is he a socialist? Not by his words. Socialism does not work, says he. So, what does he do? He gives plots of land back to the people with thirty and fifty year leases. Does a thirty year lease on land sound like ownership to you? It does to me.

Perhaps you have heard the ancient proverb: "Give a hundred year lease on a desert and people will turn it into a garden. But give a one year lease on a garden and they will turn it into a desert."

Ownership leads to better management. Ownership leads to proper stewardship. Private property is the prerequisite for freedom, and freedom is the mainspring of human progress. If you don't believe that, let me ask you a question: When was the last time that you washed a rental car?

WORLD GROWTH

It has taken from the beginning of time until now to create $25 trillion of gross world product. In thirty years, it will be nearly $50 trillion. China has been growing at 10 percent average annual rates of growth since 1978 and soon will be the second largest economy in the world. Western Europe is also growing. Eastern Europe will eventually get there. Latin and South America will be an early 21st century miracle. The Pacific Rim, with most of the world's population, will duplicate the record of Hong Kong, Taiwan, Singapore, and Japan. Freedom, private property and economic incentives are changing the way the world works. And, interestingly, the United States will be one of the main beneficiaries of that growth.

Economic trade is the great civilizer. Everybody benefits. When we exchange fabrics, we exchange ideas.

The world is a closed economy in the midst of an Information Revolution. Remarkable advances in computer technology are making capital and labor increasingly mobile. Financial capital travels around the world on an electronic highway at the speed of light. With a personal computer, a modem and a telephone, a person living in any one country is a potential employee of a company located in any other country.

It is a global economy tied together in a global network; integrated in the sense that every economic event that takes place in the world is felt somewhere else in the world. The globalization of economic markets is the most profound thing happening to business today.

The world can no longer be understood as a collection of national economies. Electronic infrastructure is creating a world-wide economy. Products have value added all over the world. The dress you buy in St. Louis may have originated with cloth woven in Korea, finished in Taiwan and cut and sewn in India. Then, there was the brief stop in Milan to pick up its *Made in Italy* label before the final journey to your store in St. Louis, the beautiful city and gateway to the West.

I was having a hot dog from a New York City street vendor and hung on his street cart was a fax machine. I said to him, "Sir, a fax machine?" He smiled and said, "Goin' global, man!"

Capital also is highly mobile. Capital does not care if it is in Tokyo or Sydney or London or New York. Capital is going to its highest and best use.

Brains are replacing BTU's. Old technologies—fossil fuels, all standard automobiles as we know them, centralized power plants and coal mines, for example, will be replaced. Minds will replace mines. Electric cars and fiber optics will redefine transportation and telecommunications. The main fuels of society such as coal, oil, gas and nuclear will be partially replaced by sunlight—the ubiquitous fuel. New technologies will constantly add new jobs to an economy that will increasingly purchase experiences rather than things. It is a world that not only offers semiconductors, but a semiconductor that is made from amorphous rather than crystalline materials. It will not only store information but actually be used as a source of energy. The photovoltaic cell made on roll to roll scrolls by robots at low temperatures and low cost compared to the crystalline photovoltaic process will literally revolutionize the way the world works and lives. All humans everywhere will take advantage of the five million quads of energy that the sun bountifully deposits on the earth each year.

The exemplary product of the Information Age is, of course, the computer. Knowledge extraction, integration and application is becoming the world's business. Knowledge is really the source of almost all economic value; the toupee that covers our baldness; the only instrument of production not subject to diminishing returns.

As oil, steel and machines once added muscle to human effort, the computer now multiplies our brain. Though our minds are limited in storing voluminous amounts of information, they are without parallel in grasping ideas and meaning. Imagine the creativity of human intelligence as it partners with a machine that can compute more in a minute than a million mathematicians in a millennia. When machines work and workers think, humans do what they do best.

How are national governments going to regulate the global economy?

They can't!

The principles of freedom, private property and the free market coupled with an intellectual system driven by knowledge and technology will render obsolete the old paradigm of extraction and central control by governments.

In the new paradigm, we must realize that the means of production in capitalism are not chiefly land, labor, and machines which traditionally have been regulated, controlled, and taxed by government, but rather emancipated human intelligence. Capitalism, the mind-centered system, finds the driving force of its growth is innovation and discovery. Governments must let go of their nonsensical, paternalistic control over people. So must corporations. So must we all.

The growing global economy enhances the importance of economic trade while reducing the influence of politics and control. Economic competition is slowly replacing political confrontation. Although the political map has boundaries, the competitive map of financial and industrial activity does not.

THE U.S. SURGE

What in the world is going on? Freedom, privatization, and unbelievable economic growth. Interestingly, the United States will be one of the main beneficiaries of globalization. World growth and competition has convinced American firms that a set of written rules and company procedures passed through a hierarchy of managers is inefficient. Command and control structures do not work with countries or companies. If there is one economic lesson we should learn after the fall of the

Berlin Wall, it is that socialists could not make socialism work and neither can capitalists.

Realizing that top-down, rigid, hierarchical structures of decision making are too slow and cumbersome, successful companies are making a major change. They are decentralizing. Customer-oriented American firms are remaking themselves into fast changing, flexible, and adaptive organisms. Caught in the vortex of change and world competition, corporate bureaucracy is being dismantled. Management is getting tough on its competition and easy on its people. Self-managing work teams are being empowered through employee involvement in decision making. Everyone is given an opportunity to improve the process by putting responsibility and authority into the hands of those closest to the customer. It is a way of thinking that focuses first on people, then on organizations, then on things.

Although decentralization has paid off for most, not all sectors are moving in that direction. Recent media and telecommunication mergers apparently are an attempt to buck the trend and create an information highway in record time. Time will tell if centralization in those industries works. For the moment, at least, they believe it is easier to ride the horse in the direction it is already headed.

U.S. VERSUS THE WORLD

Many people think that Japan has a higher standard of living than the United States and that Germany and France are very close. They reach this conclusion by comparing per capita output in each country, then converting it to a common currency, such as the dollar.

However, simply converting to a common currency does not give a clear picture, because the purchasing power of the same amount of output differs in each country. It takes considerable more minutes of work to buy a pound of beef, a new car, or a house in Japan and Germany than it does in the United States.

Based on exchange rates, Japan's per capita output exceeded the U.S.'s by 20 percent in 1988. However, a comparison of purchasing power shows that Japan's per capita output was actually more than 20 percent below the U.S. level. Based on exchange rates, Germany's per capita output equaled the U.S.'s in 1988. In terms of purchasing power, Germany's per capita output was about 15 percent below the U.S. level.

The gap has narrowed over the last forty years. But this is due to exceptionally high growth in other countries, particularly Japan and Germany, not to low growth in the U.S.

Further, the U.S. savings rate is ready to take off. We have been a low saving country. Japan has been a high saving country. There are, of course, many cultural and institutional reasons. Demographics is now emerging as an important force determining savings. Japan, in the past twenty-five years, has had most of its population in the age brackets of forty, fifty and sixty years old. That is the time when most people save. The U.S., in turn, had its population mainly in their teens, twenties and thirties. Americans gave birth to seventy-five million post World War II baby boomers, four million babies each year from

1948 to 1965. They are just now entering their forties. For most people, savings takes priority after the age of forty.

Until then, the needs are mostly "feed me, house me, clothe me, entertain me, and educate me." Visualize it this way: seventy-five million people all saying "serve me." Believe it or not, the boomers will now make significant contributions to our economy as they move into the high saving and productive stage of their lives.

Savings rates should start going up and keep increasing for the next thirty years. If that is true, the future is ours. Economic growth, after all, is critically linked to savings and investment.

English is emerging as the universal language. What a competitive advantage that will be.

Seventy percent of the world's software writers reside in the United States. The most important source of new wealth will be knowledge—information times work equals value.

The United States has the best transportation system in the world for both people and goods. Despite the great distance, it costs an American far less to travel or ship a product from New York to California, for example, than it does his European counterpart to travel or ship a fraction of that distance.

The United States has approximately 1.5 million retail stores selling hundreds of thousands of different types of goods. Our system of distributing goods from the factory to the consumer is the best in the free world by a wide margin and a major contributor to our world economic power status.

The United States today has approximately 400,000 restaurants offering so many varieties of food and such a wide range of prices that Americans eat almost half their meals outside of the home.

U.S. MANUFACTURING REGAINS THE LEAD

The McKenzie Global Institute released a two and a half year study in 1992 that emphasizes the U.S. is now number one in manufacturing in most categories: aeronautics, basic materials, beverages, chemicals, food, paper, plastics, petroleum telecommunications, wood, semiconductors, and soon to be number one in high definition television. Freedom works.

On average, a full-time American worker produced $49,600 in goods and services in 1990. The country closest to the United States was France, with $47,000 per worker, or 95 percent of U.S. productivity. Japan produced $38,200 per worker, 77 percent of the U.S. figure. West Germany produced $44,200 per worker and the United Kingdom $37,100, which equals 89 percent and 75 percent of U.S. productivity respectively.

One reason the U.S. is first is because of more internal competition and freer markets. German and Japanese factory workers produced just 80 percent as much, on average, as American workers on an hourly basis. Japan's total manufacturing productivity is lower mainly because of the very weak productivity in Japanese industries that sell mostly at home. Although the U.S. leads in manufacturing productivity, it is farthest ahead in the service sector, which now employs three out of four American workers.

The most important factor in determining productivity for a specific industry is how much freedom countries allow for competitors to enter the market and to offer services at unrestricted prices. For example, general merchandise retailing is more than twice as efficient in the United States as in Japan, largely because Japan's zoning laws protect small stores.

The deregulated American telecommunications industry is at least twice as productive as Germany's government monopoly. Competition always produces efficiency and lower prices.

AGRICULTURE: FREEDOM, PROPERTY RIGHTS AND INFORMATION

When I was a young boy growing up on a farm, we worked hard. The land was fenced. Private property provided a tremendous incentive. What was grown, harvested and sold was ours. Taxes at that time were less than five cents for every dollar earned.

We would use a small tractor a dozen times on each field for one crop. In the spring, we would cover the field with manure using a spreader. Then we would plow; then disk; then harrow; then float the field; then plant the field; then cultivate the field at least three times to kill weeds and make the furrows for irrigating. Last, we would harvest the crop. The point is that a person would drive a tractor through the field many times to grow and harvest a crop.

Today, modern farmers might drive the tractor through the field to plant and harvest. That's it. Fifty years ago one farmer could grow enough to feed between twenty and thirty people; that number today is currently 128 and continues to grow.

In the beginning, farmers had muscle. Then, they had machinery. And unlike many farmers throughout the world, American farmers always had property rights, freedom and the incentive to produce. Now, in another quantum leap, they have PC's and information.

Farmers used to guess how much their farms would yield. Today, Massey Ferguson has a yield mapping system that can help the farmer maximize the yield on each square yard in every single field.

The system links the farmer's tractor to a satellite-based global positioning system which positions and records the latitude, longitude and yield of every square yard of soil. Then data goes to the farmer's desktop computer which can be used to investigate selected areas and pinpoint the reasons for the differences in yield. Soil impaction, nutrient imbalance, types of hybrid seed, water requirements and many other factors would then be looked at to see if it is economical to implement yield enhancing remedies.

The result of America's agricultural miracle?

The food production industries, including farming, manufacturing, distribution, marketing and sales, produce 16 percent of our nation's GDP and provide one out of every six jobs in the U.S. The industry generates twenty-one million jobs, or about 17 percent of the entire U.S. work force. Nearly 90 percent of those jobs are located off the farm. Total consumer expenditures for food last year totaled $503 billion, with $315 billion spent on food in grocery stores and the remainder spent on eating establishments and other retail outlets. Americans spend less of their disposable income on food (10 percent) than do most of the world's consumers (14 percent in Europe,

28 percent in Russia, 48 percent in China, and 53 percent in India). As food takes less and less of our disposable income, we have more discretionary income to spend on other things. The jobs of the future will be in those "other things."

As agriculture becomes more productive using machinery, hybrid seeds and information, a relatively small number of farmers are able to grow enough food for everybody in the U.S. as well as a substantial part of the rest of the world. Increases in agricultural productivity release farmers to do other kinds of jobs. And just as we could not predict where all the buggy whip makers would work with the advent of the "horseless carriage," neither can we know where everybody will work in the future. But count on it. There will be good jobs.

This Information Revolution represents the most radical period of change since the Industrial Revolution. Individuals will get to use their minds, as well as their muscles. Machines work. People think.

PART II

WHAT IN THE U.S. IS GOING ON?

Chapter Four

THE INFORMATION ECONOMY

"Capitalism, or the market economy, or the free enterprise system—whatever you choose to label it—was not planned. Like life on earth, it need not be. Capitalism just happened and it will keep on happening. Quite spontaneously. Capitalism flourishes whenever it is not suppressed, because it is a naturally occurring phenomenon. It is the way human society organizes itself for survival in a world of limited resources."

So begins *Bionomics* by Michael Rothschild. Shattering the paradigm "society as machine" and replacing it with "society as a living thing," Rothschild, like Ludwig von Mises, changes forever the way people will think about business, markets and everyday life.

Unfortunately, most economists and politicians want the power of control. They assume technology constant, preach equilibrium economics, and invoke fiscal and monetary policy to "run" the economy. For them, the economy is static, predictable and manageable.

But the world is now in the throes of an epochal transformation—moving away from the Machine Age and into the Information Age; from models based on physics to those based on biology. The economy as machine will not suffice.

Instead, the economy is a living social organism where the beneficial outcomes generated by a spontaneous free market order cannot be known in advance, nor can it be planned. The self-regulating nature of a market economy is comparable to the interdependent qualities of a rain forest's ecosystem. It is a self-organizing information system that thrives on change and organizational learning.

F. A. Hayek insisted that the market economy is the most complicated phenomenon on earth and therefore very unpredictable. Unintended consequences, he wrote in *The Fatal Conceit*, are paramount. The fatal conceit is the presumption that governments or economists can manage the economy.

Economic incentives and the price system work so well that, for the most part, we are unaware of their influence. The market works until it is prevented from working. Government passes laws, rules, regulations, taxes and imposes tariffs. Then, when the market responds like a drunken sailor, governments impose price controls and ration stamps.

When light supplies loomed extra tight
and candles flickered in the night,
Tom tinkered with his bulbs so bright.

— Meanwhile —

Less enlightened folk on a different kick,
clamored for the government to ration
all the candlewick.

Ration stamps, they promised,
will light the darkest hour,
by making sure, both rich and poor,
share what's left of candlepower.

But stubborn Tom just tinkered on,
and with his bulbs and lamps,
he licked the curse of darkness
while dimwits licked their ration stamps!

Fortunately, the world is still basking in the afterglow of Edison. Aren't you glad he was a tinkerer and not a politician?

Even if government could make prudent calculations and issue the right amount of ration stamps at the right price, they simply could not predict all the behavioral changes that would follow.

Modern, complex economies require mechanisms to coordinate human action. The free-market economic system is the only known means capable of gathering the special knowledge of specific time and place. Its language is price, wage, interest rate, profit and loss, which tell buyers and sellers the costs and benefits of their actions. Nobody plans it. The market just happens. Markets are an irreplaceable signaling system analogous to the thermostatic control for your home heating system. Changes in the market's underlying costs—resource supplies and consumer demands—are quickly disseminated through changing market prices. Behaviors are altered. A Brazilian freeze, for example, signals reduced coffee bean supplies, the price of coffee rises, and coffee drinkers, finding their coffee more expensive, restrain consumption. The shortages eventually go away as buyers and sellers keep adjusting their behavior.

Scarcity always leads to reduced consumption, the discovery of substitutes, and the improvement of productivity. How else could we have gone from candles to whale oil, to petroleum, to electricity? Human beings are purposeful, goal-oriented, rational beings who act from enlightened self-interest. They do not have to be taught economics before they can make choices. Every person makes individual choices, and while they have different views on what they want to produce, consume, and trade, they all follow the same predictable laws of economics and nature. Information is the essence of both systems. Biological systems follow the genetic information contained in DNA. Economic systems follow the technological information and price signals generated by the know-how of the billions of people living on this planet.

Scientists have finally accepted the idea that the natural world runs itself without the help of man. Now, the economic planners, social engineers, and governmentalists of all stripes must do the same with the economic world. Leave it alone. Bug out. Government is a parasite that destroys its host. We must remember that businesses create prosperity while governments try to take the credit.

Protesting the market is about as useful as protesting gravity. Fighting a natural phenomena is a waste of time and energy.

The market is! Gravity is! While many planners think they are fighting an ideology, they are, in fact, fighting a first principle. The market, like gravity, represents the natural order of things. You don't have to plan the market, manage the market or control the market. Capitalism happens. And it will keep on happening.

Enlightened self-interest cannot be extinguished. Profit seeking is a self organizing mechanism that emerges spontaneously from mutually beneficial relationships based on mutual profitability. Without planning or direction, the market communicates and coordinates widely dispersed knowledge for rapid adaptation to the changing circumstances of time and place.

It does so on a mind-boggling scale. It works because it lets people do well by doing good. The market acts as a constant flushing mechanism, winnowing out both your follies and mine.

INSTITUTIONAL COLLAPSE/INDIVIDUAL TRIUMPH

As computers evolve, centralized power dissolves. The microchip never met a bureaucratic job it didn't like.

Almost overnight the U.S. went from the Machine Age to the Information Age, from big time CEO's to no-name entrepreneurs, from an economy that resembled a machine to one that resembles an ecosystem that is far too complex to be designed or controlled by planners.

This section about the United States describes the dying horses and emerging steeds of this epochal transformation.

U.S. companies have reinvented themselves using PC's, voice mail, e-mail, fax machines, cellular phones, local area networks, satellite uplinks and other technologies to boost quality, increase service, cut costs, improve response time and accelerate responsiveness. Today's management is about liberating people.

Individuals will work in the contract society as internal functions are contracted out to take full advantage of the opportunities in the marketplace.

Schooling will be transformed because of competition. Parents will have choice. Students will be empowered. Technology will render the educational hierarchy obsolete as government schools are toppled by market alternatives.

Big governments will crumble. For the first time in world history, we may have governance without government. Governments, like carburetors, are becoming irrelevant.

Chapter Five

LIBERATING THE ORGANIZATION

"The lumbering bureaucracies of this century," says Texas Instruments' Steve Pruitt and Electronic Data Systems' Tom Barrett, in their new book *Cyberspace: First Steps*, "will be replaced by fluid, interdependent groups of problem solvers."

"But how do you do that?" you might ask. Their answer: Don't sweat it. It will happen. People organize themselves. Order happens. Leaves are green. "Self-organizing, interdependent groups will become pervasive in these times of constant change," they say.

Another important book making a similar point is Meg Wheatley's *Leadership and the New Science*. Her book is music to a free market economist's ears. In a business organization, she explains, "order is." Busy people are smarter than the fastest machines. Writes Wheatley,

> Forget re-engineering. What is re-engineering but another attempt, usually by the people at the top, to impose new structures over old—to take one set of rigid rules and guidelines and impose them on the rest of the organization.

It is a mechanical view of organizations and people—that you can "design" a perfect solution and then the machine will comply with this new set of instructions. . . . Re-engineering does not change what needs to be changed most: the way people at all levels relate to the enterprise. We need to be asking: Has the organization's capacity to change increased and improved? Or, have we just created a new structure that will atrophy as the environment shifts?

Just as centralism does not work with government, hierarchical structures do not work with business. Top down, command and control mechanisms are now dysfunctional.

By examining the five competitive strategies that have driven corporations in this century, we can see how the revolutionary forces of information and organizational change will determine the future of the American business environment.

SIZE

In the early 1900s, corporate industrialists were interested in market share, increased volumes and batch process. Henry Ford's assembly line was a good example. Corporations were committed to size, volume and large market shares.

EFFICIENCY

Then, the emphasis shifted to reducing costs and improving profit margins. Time-motion studies, a method of management that centered on classifying and streamlining individual movements for maximum efficiency, were wide spread. In addition, vertical integration to control efficiencies top to bottom were installed. The goal was to be the low cost provider.

QUALITY

The quality movement followed. The Japanese learned about TQM in the 1950s and began instituting its processes in the 1960s and 70s. While U.S. firms were busy producing in quantity, with little concern for quality, American professors Deming and Juran were lecturing the Japanese on Total Quality Management.

Nothing attracts customers like service and quality, they argued. But, for quality to be a system and not just a slogan, it must be measured. Just-in-time inventory control (JIT), statistical process control (SPC), and all kinds of mathematical, managerial and statistical techniques were brought to bear on measuring customer service, employee satisfaction and cash flow. Improve quality by improving the process. Measurement, among other things, is a source of ideas to track progress. Quality is not *a* competitive edge, it is *the* competitive edge. All processes are vulnerable to the loss of quality through variation. If the levels of variation are managed, however, they can be decreased and quality can be raised. Company-wide quality management, CWQM, is the goal.

U.S. firms began their quality move in the early 1980s, and by the last half of the decade had caught up with the Japanese. The practice of TQM and continual improvement maintains the United States status as the most productive manufacturing economy in the world.

A quick story to illustrate how we did it.

Two moose hunters went to Alaska to hunt moose. Their pilot told them he was on a tight schedule and that after their hunt they should be ready to depart at a certain place and time.

The plane arrived on schedule. The hunters loaded their gear, guns, and made preparations to take off.

"Did you load our moose?" they asked the pilot.

The dumfounded pilot questioned, "You shot a moose?"

The hunters replied, "No, we each shot a moose."

The pilot snorted, "Why, if we load those moose on this plane we will never get off the water."

The hunters indignantly looked at him and insisted, "We did it last year."

The pilot asked, "You did?"

So, they got out of the plane, loaded a moose on each pontoon, taxied to the end of the lake, revved the engines, released, and let 'er go. Faster, faster, faster, finally to the edge of the lake and barely lifting off the water, . . . Wham! They hit a tree. There was airplane and moose meat every where.

One of the hunters, on his knees in the mud, yelled "Joe, Joe, where are we?"

Joe yelled back from his perch high in a tree, "From what I can tell, fifty feet farther than last year."

Companies today have taken the moral of that story one better; fifty feet farther each day, every day. Good enough never is. When it comes to service and quality, there is no finish line. You can never stop thinking about it.

RESPONSE TIME

The fourth phase of corporate competitive evolution was response time. Quick, fast, and flexible. Frito-Lay, as one example, involved itself in a fundamental rethinking and a radical redesign of every aspect of their business to achieve dramatic performance levels and improve service. The company implemented a new scheme for pricing and promotion, added new products, developed a technological inventory management system, and gave the sales force hand-held computers. Inefficiency was the enemy. Response time was the new goal. The race is no longer between the large and the small—it is between the fast and the slow. Guess who wins?

Federal Express, with its 10:30 a.m. "absolutely, positively overnight" delivery service, made us believe everyone should behave this way. Now, when a customer places an order, when do they expect it? That's right. Tomorrow morning, ten thirty.

Federal Express not only insists on quick, on-time delivery, but they also want to be perceived that way. Every day they spend an estimated $26,000 to steam wash their internationally recognized red, violet, and white trucks to make sure the company maintains its visual impact.

In short, we have entered what the Wall Street Journal calls the Nimble World—where enterprises must have the ability and willingness to navigate at warp speed through a constantly shifting meteor shower of products, consumer whims and competitors.

Another story: Each morning in Africa a lion awakens and realizes he has to out run the slowest gazelle. In turn, every day a gazelle gets up and realizes he must out run the fastest lion. The moral of the story? No matter who you are, when you get up, you better start running.

SURPRISE AND DELIGHT

Today, the corporate challenge is to exceed customers' expectations. Quality? Yes. Service? Yes. Response time? Yes. But now you must be customer obsessed and consumer-centric. Products and services must go beyond people's expectations. Customers no longer want to talk about how a product works or discuss its outstanding features. They either say "I love it," or they don't. If they don't, you're done.

A personal example: I am flying from Phoenix to Dallas on American Airlines. The air is rougher than I have ever experienced. Everybody is getting sick.

Seated in Row 2, I notice a woman in a front row bulkhead window seat get white as a sheet. Gagging, she pops her seat belt to step across the man next to her to go to the bathroom. As she takes her first step, she throws up on his lap.

The flight attendant immediately gets up and helps the lady into the bathroom. The attendant quickly gathers some paper towels and goes to help the man clean his lap. As the flight attendant bends down to help the poor man, she too gags. Wham. His lap is heaved on again. I mean, it is the funniest thing I've ever seen in my life. Two times in less than a minute.

The man unbuckles his seat belt, stands up, turns around, and says to everybody in first class, "Would anyone else like to throw up on my lap?"

It was a stitch.

I give him my business card and ask him to let me know how this all comes out, so to speak.

A month later, he writes and says American Airlines gave him money for a new suit and two free first class air tickets to any destination.

Now, that's what I call "surprise and delight."

Most companies are catching on. Be consumer-centric. Get in the consumer's shoes. "Don't tell me about your grass seed. Tell me about my lawn."

The interesting thing about the service economy is that there is nothing tangible. You can't demonstrate it, inspect it, warehouse it, recall it, or store it. As Charles Revlon once said, "We manufacture perfume in the factory, but we sell hope in the store." Charles Ritz was reported to have said, "The guest is always right. The guest is always right. Even if you have to throw him out of the hotel, the guest is always right."

Total quality, excellence, empowerment, innovation, flexibility, self-directed work teams, continual improvement and bench-marking are just a few of the paths leading to the same destination: Serving the customer.

WHAT DOES IT ALL MEAN?

For some companies, it has been a long, arduous road. Think for a minute about the situations in which many of you have been involved.

Yes, business must be given extensive freedom of action to ensure profits and employment. Yet, many times, the explanation of how wonderfully the market works stops short when it comes to employees. Inside many of our companies, the heavy, visible hand of management is far too prevalent.

They rule, command and control.

The regimentation of work has produced employees whose habits and thinking stem from a work situation of subordination. How can the average worker ever hope to see the value of independence and self-propulsion when he or she is managed by a command and control mentality? In hierarchical structures, people tend to become the way they work: politicized, petty and passive.

Information and globalization, however, will encourage an enlightened leadership that will de-politicize the work place, empower individuals and encourage self supervision. Success will go to those who structure for constant improvement and can make constant change. Firms organized along horizontal, fast, cross-functional, and cooperative lines will outperform those who regiment, subordinate, and control

In short, the best big companies will behave like the best small companies.

PEOPLE ARE THE KEY

The challenge of the nineties will be to unleash entrepreneurial centers of opportunity throughout the organization.

The instantaneous transmission of information and availability of data to those at every level of authority makes human intelligence and intellectual resources a company's main source of wealth.

Successful companies will be those that emphasize ideas, innovation, and growth as much as operational efficiency. They will see themselves as architects designing the future rather than engineers preserving the past.

The logic goes like this: the revolution in information and communications technology makes knowledge the new competitive resource. But knowledge only flows through the technology. It actually resides in people; in knowledge-workers, and in the organizations they inhabit. The manager's job is to create an environment that allows knowledge-workers to learn from their own experiences, from each other, and from customers, suppliers and business partners. It is everybody's job to help people convert data into information, information into knowledge and, most importantly, knowledge into action and sales that serve customers.

Business is about communication. It is the skill through which results are produced. It touches and is touched, is dispersed but interconnected, reaches out and is reached for, moves and is moved upon. Communication will not connect two points. It must connect all points.

In the new economy, Peter Drucker argues, knowledge is not just another resource alongside the traditional factors of production—labor, land, and capital. It is the only meaningful resource today. An organization is always in competition for its most essential resource: qualified, knowledgeable and dedicated people who work in an environment of continual learning, becoming more valuable.

Today, there is a fundamental tension between knowledge-workers and the organizations in which they work. On the one hand, knowledge-workers are independent. They, not the company, own the means of production—their knowledge. And they can walk out the door at any moment. Thus, it becomes the job of the company to market itself to its employees. Managers have to attract and motivate the best people; reward, recognize, and retain them; train, educate and improve them; and in the most remarkable reversal of all, serve and satisfy them.

Once, it was working for IBM and becoming an IBMer. Now, every company must adapt to its employees.

The secret is to understand what people really want out of their jobs and give it to them. Some have it backwards. Instead of concentrating on what is expected from their employees, companies should concentrate on what their employees expect from them.

Empowering people comes from an understanding that the emotions and feelings that drive people in their personal lives are the same forces that motivate them in their jobs. People want to be challenged. They thrive on responsibility, enjoy recognition and welcome opportunity. Everyone wants to be appreciated.

In an age of information and empowerment, it is futile to try to organize people. Organize work? Yes. Organize people? No. Trying to organize people will inevitably create the opposite of what was intended. Chaos rather than order. Boredom instead of efficiency. Bureaucracy rather than flexibility. Constraint rather than growth.

It has always been possible to buy a person's hands. In a world where machines work and people think, however, we need their ideas on streamlining the workplace. Energizing people must spring from an empowering philosophy of life, giving them the chance to personally make a difference. It adheres to principles that are consistent with life itself—freedom, growth, and choice.

Individuals do not want to work for companies.
They want to work for movements,
for causes, for dreams.

Individuals do not want to work for companies. They want to work for movements, for causes, for dreams. Martin Luther King said "I have a dream." He said nothing about a strategic plan. Ronald Reagan had a vision. "What brought America back? The American people brought us back—with quiet courage and common sense; with undying faith that in this nation under God, the future will be ours; for the future belongs to the free." Jack Welch, CEO of General Electric, says his goal is to create an "effervescent culture just crackling with creativity."

In a sense then, there is no management model, only people. The model is to pay attention to people. What is holding them back? What is frustrating them? What is restraining them? In short, what is depriving them of a rich, rewarding, forceful, and energized effort?

Tom Peters, in an *ASAP* magazine article, reports the following. On October 21, 1993, the $300 million Rockport Company shut down entirely to conduct an all hands strategy retreat. There was no agenda. They were told to invent their own meeting. Slowly, but surely, each person who wished to do so would step into the center of the circle of all Rockport employees gathered in a warehouse and name a topic about which he felt passionate enough to lead a breakout session. They would write their topic on a large sheet of paper and stick it to the wall with masking tape. They would continue until nobody had any additional items to post. Then, the "market place" would open and people would sign up for as many sessions as they could for that day. Participants who posted issues would be responsible for the meeting, facilitating the discussion and recording minutes of the proceedings.[1]

If you believe that order happens, then you are comfortable with these principles: whoever comes, comes; whatever happens is the only thing that could happen; whenever it starts is the right time; and when it's over, it's over. If anyone was bored, not learning anything, or felt they had nothing to contribute, they could just walk away.

In less than an hour dozens of issues were posted. The meeting featured some 66 sessions with 5 to 150 participants each. Everybody agreed the meeting was a smashing success. Follow-up led to significant progress and a positive shift in the overall attitude in the company was noted in company surveys measuring employee satisfaction.

It is every individual's responsibility to make themselves more valuable. Great work environments harbor no secrets. Skills should be upgraded through intense and continuous training, as well as through the kind of meetings just described. Although lifetime employment is highly unlikely, through constant training and education, everyone can be prepared for lifetime employability.

General Electric, in the early 1980s would take three weeks after an order to deliver a custom-made circuit-breaker box. Now it takes three days. Similarly, Motorola would turn out electronic pagers three weeks after the factory got the order. Now it does it in two hours. AT&T used to require two years to design a new phone. Now they aim for six months.

Although lifetime employment is highly unlikely, through constant training and education, everyone can be prepared for lifetime employability.

How did it happen? Because management invested in people, empowered them, and believed that self-organization in widely distributed systems are the essence of innovation and progress.

When I worked with John Kotter, famous for his books *The Leadership Factor* and *A Force for Change*, on a telecommunications conference in Alabama, he told me about the studies of two colleagues, Jim Kesket and Leonard Schlesinger at the Harvard Business School. In particular, they found companies that have distinguished themselves in the ways they hire, train and treat their employees have experienced significant increases in service quality and customer satisfaction. They have also experienced growth rates two to three times greater than their competitors.

These results stem primarily from improvements in employee retention and productivity, which directly impacts customer retention.

No surprise. It stems from leadership that invests in people and then lets them organize themselves. Treat people like owners and they begin to act like owners.

James A. Belasco and Ralph C. Stayer make an important point in their book *Flight of the Buffalo:*

For a long time, I believed the old leadership paradigm that told me that my job was to plan, organize, command, coordinate, and control. I saw my organization functioning like a herd of buffalo. Buffalo are absolutely loyal followers of one leader. They do whatever the leader wants them to do, go wherever the leader wants them to go. I realized eventually that my organization didn't work as well as I'd like, because buffalo are loyal to one leader; they stand around and wait for the leader to show them what to do. When the leader isn't around, they wait for him to show up . . . People did only what I told them to do, and then they waited around for my next set of instructions.

I also found it was hard work being the lead buffalo. Giving all the orders, doing all the "important" work took 12-14 hours a day. Meanwhile my company was getting slaughtered out there in the market place because I couldn't respond quickly enough to changes.

Then one day I got it. What I really wanted in the organization was a group of responsible interdependent workers, similar to a flock of geese. I could see the geese flying in their "V" formation, the leadership changing frequently, with different geese taking the lead. I saw every goose being responsible for getting itself to wherever the gaggle was going, changing roles whenever necessary, alternating as a leader, a follower, or a scout. And when the task changed, the geese would be responsible for changing the structure of the group to accommodate, similar to the geese that fly in a "V" but land in waves. I could see each goose being a leader.

Then I saw clearly that the biggest obstacle to success was my picture of a loyal herd of buffalo waiting for me, the leader, to tell them what to do. I knew I had to change the picture to become a different kind of leader, so everyone could become a leader."

Ninety-nine percent of all employees want to do a good job—whether they do or not depends to a large degree on who they work for and how their work is organized. Largely a symbolic activity, management involves energizing people to levels they did not think possible. High expectations produce high results. Everyone should be given a chance to lead.

ORGANIZING THE ORGANIZATION

American firms are realizing that a set of written rules and company procedures passed through a hierarchy of managers does not produce enough leaders or innovation. Companies are so strapped with rules and traditions, and bound in government laws that even top management does not have to lead anyone anywhere. They simply follow precedents, obey regulations, and lead in the sense that the carved wooden figurehead leads the ship.

Command and control structures of hierarchical organizations are simply out of synchronization with an information economy that must respond quickly to change. Doing the right job as well as the job done right thrives in an atmosphere where people motivate themselves.

Hierarchies rank, rule, and regiment work. Interdependence encourages, affirms and releases.

Hierarchies hire people. Empowering people enlists their support.

Hierarchies look to management consultants. Leaders ask those involved with the task for their ideas.

Hierarchies view people as extensions of their machines. Liberated minds see independence and self propulsion as the best way to perform multiple tasks and function as a contributing member of a team.

Empowering people creates a climate of innovation and achievement because it fosters relationships of belonging and family. Many of the rigid rules that seem to multiply in large companies are no longer effective. Rules passed through a hierarchy of managers cannot adjust spontaneously to circumstances that are changing at ever rapid rates.

People working in hierarchies often do not tell management there is a better way. They assume that is the way management wants it.

ORGANIZING SO PEOPLE CAN ORGANIZE

Every company in America will one day realize that self-organization in widely distributed systems is the essence of innovation and progress. When the business environment shifts, people will shift. This kind of organization will thrive, not atrophy.

Kevin Kelly is another articulate champion of the biological, self-organizing approach. His new book, *Out of Control: The Rise of Neo-Biological Civilization*, clearly enunciates the Nine Laws of God. His first: "Distribute being. . . . Whenever we find something from nothing we find it arising from a field of many interacting pieces. All the mysteries we find most interesting, such as life and intelligence, are found in the soil of large distributed systems."

The Internet is an example of where one new network is being added every 10 minutes and is the essence, really, of innovation, progress and life itself. Tom Peters writes, "These are eternal ideas—and ideas whose time has come. The flavor of the new, dispersed but interconnected, self-designing world of commerce is here. It's time to throw away the engineering and re-engineering texts," he says, "and acquire a biology library instead. Welcome to the world of anti-entropy and self organization."

Eleven-year-old Anna Paquin captures the idea in her award winning commercial for MCI.

There will be a road.

It will not connect two points.

It will connect all points.

Its speed limit will be the speed of light.

It will not go from here to there.

We will all only be here.

Chapter Six

INDIVIDUALS AND THE CONTRACT SOCIETY

Machine Age America offered workers a social contract of employment: work hard and you will have a job for life. If layoffs become necessary, you'll probably be rehired. Employees enjoyed a degree of security in their insecurity.

Today is different. Employees constantly hear that "people are a company's most important asset," but what they see is that people are the most expendable asset. For example, 1993 saw large companies announcing nearly 600,000 layoffs. Now, if you are laid off from your mid-management position, you have reason to believe you will never be hired back into that or any other white-collar job. A highly competitive, globalized economy has completely transformed the realities of the market place. The man with the clipboard who makes sure the widgets are in the right place in the factory at the right time is replaced by some technological gadget. Your company just does not need you anymore.

Or, as the cartoon in the *Wall Street Journal* of one employee talking to another after a chat with the boss, "He didn't exactly say I was doing a good job, but he did say that I'm the least of his worries."

Changing technologies, in blunt terms, caused the off-loading of most physical and repetitive tasks to the computer. Computers are the machines of the mind that free us from the drudgery of information processing. But, as the drudgery vanishes, so do some of the drudges. Blue collar. White collar. Ring around the collar. No matter.

Management guru Peter Drucker predicts that by the year 2000, two-thirds of the management positions that existed in the late 1980s will have been wiped out.

Work reality is now different. Life used to be linear: birth, education, work for 30 years, gold watch, retire, and die. But now the cycle of education/training—job, quit for a new job or be fired and forced to find a new job—is followed by more training, more education, work for five years or so, and then, you guessed it: quit for a new job or be fired and forced to go through the whole cycle again. Life is circular and uncertain. It will, however, be more entrepreneurial, challenging, and here is the main point. There will be plenty of jobs.

THE CONTRACT SOCIETY

Businesses of the future will be radically downsized. The trend, in fact, will be down to one. Wealth used to be factories in the hands of a few. Today, it is information in the minds of everybody. Everyone will be an entrepreneur; everyone has a shot at the brass ring.

Business will be a move away from buildings, toward relationships and towards the customer. The signature office buildings of large corporations will give way to technologically connected spaces: cars, small offices, and homes. Subdivisions of companies will be free to buy services or products from each other or to buy from outsiders. Rather than being shielded from outside competitive pressures, subdivisions of companies will become part of the marketplace. The process of bringing an outside market into the firm will not be limited to large units of major companies. Subdivisions of subdivisions will also be forced to compete. Since the smallest subdivision is the individual, eventually we will reach a point where there is very little difference between an employee and an independent contractor. Our hierarchical business world will be replaced by a contractual society in which every individual will be in business for himself. Or, at the very least, running a business within a business.

Eventually we will reach a point where there is very little difference between an employee and an independent contractor. Our hierarchical business world will be replaced by a contractual society in which every individual will be in business for himself.

For example, in any business that has a marketing department, the president faces all of the problems of the traditional business manager: How to motivate? How to spur creativity? How to make personal goals consistent with corporate goals? How to increase sales with less budget?

In a business that contracts out for marketing services, however, the problems are quite different. Likely, there are numerous competitors who approach the manager periodically with ideas on how to better market the company's products. In the first instance, the manager asks: "How can I get other people to solve my problems?" In the second instance, the contracted, outsourced business, the question is: "How do I choose among many competitors, each of whom desperately wants to solve my problems?" In one case, employee behavior is a problem requiring "management skills" because employees are shielded from competition. In the other case, most of the traditional management problems have vanished, precisely because there is competition.

Companies will increasingly contract out internal functions and take full advantage of the opportunities created in the marketplace.

Seen in this light, it is a wonder why any company has its own marketing department, or any other internal department for that matter. Stockholders and owners will increasingly say, "Prove to me it can't be subcontracted!" Already we have computer companies that do not make computers, shoe companies that do not manufacture shoes, and bus companies that do not own buses. Companies will increasingly contract out internal functions and take full advantage of the opportunities created in the marketplace.

In the contract society, outsourcing is an opportunity for a company or entrepreneur to utilize the resources, expertise, and specialization of another company. Understanding outsourcing as a rich, new resource opens up a whole world of possibilities. Each of us must ask: "Am I working on non-strategic business functions that drain my energies and resources and, therefore, detract from my ability to achieve my strategic goals?" "Is there another company with whom I can partner to accomplish those goals so that I can focus?"

Teams, strategic alliances, individual entrepreneurs, joint ventures, open-systems, multi-vendors, inter-dependencies, partnerships—these are the words of the contract society, and the way business will be done in the future. There will be jobs, unique niches, and opportunities everywhere.

Nomads, rangers, astronauts and road warriors are just some of the new words to describe what we will do.

The virtual office is coming. There is a difference between a place called office and the activity called office work. It is a business strategy that allows people to work wherever and whenever they work best. Most will prefer their homes.

BIOLOGY AS A MODEL

Just as our understanding of the economy evolves from machine to organism, from physics to biology, so too will our understanding of business. Soon, business schools will be studying biologically based models which view the organization as a living, dynamic organism.

In biological systems, order is free. It is natural. The big rain cloud, for example, that you have watched move through the sky, suspending fifty million gallons of water in mid-air happens without a plan and without a single organizational chart.

Nature already does what business would like to do. As you look at a stream, with its silt, grass, water, fish life, rocks, nooks, crannies, and pools you witness an incredible system of flexibility and adaptability. Chaos in its parts. But, pattern and predictability as a whole.

Rigid and hierarchical business systems that make people function as cogs of a machine no longer work in the age of information and empowerment.

Successful business will tend toward flexibility and capacity for change. And just as natural systems continually renew and revitalize themselves, so must we do the same.

Instead of trying to shut down the chaos,
we must allow it to become part of a process
that moves us to new levels of order.

Life, like nature, is chaotic. But over the long term, chaos has patterns. In natural systems, order develops from within. "Order is. Order happens," says management consultant Meg Wheatley.

All of us have dark times, tunnel times, chaotic times. Broken relationships, illness, grief and death are, in the words of Forrest Gump's mommy, "just a part of livin'."

But, like nature, we must let go of those times. And as we do, we come out with a greater sense of purpose. Instead of trying to shut down the chaos, we must allow it to become part of a process that moves us to new levels of order.

Do something. Do anything. Many a false step is taken by just standing still. Take risk. Corporate chaos is here to stay. Broaden your skills. Branch out. Build new skills. Moonlight and learn. Work on your resume. Always carry business cards—pass them out whenever you can. Know a head hunter. Have an escape hatch. Educate and re-educate yourself. Job security does not exist anymore. You are never too old to change, learn something new, or start over. Personal initiative, responsibility and the ability to explore options are now the requirements needed to succeed in the marketplace.

Value will come from what you know and what you have access to, not where you are.

New skills are required. Upgrading technology must be superseded by upgrading people. Personal goals used to include job security. Now they must include job adaptability. Yesterday, promotion was by seniority. Today, it is by performance. Our parents thought retirement. We must think re-engagement.

COMMUNICATION AND THE CONTRACT SOCIETY

Patterns of communication are also altered. Since information is power, it was something to be closely guarded. Now, information is the source of all change, and everyone must have access to it. It is information that forms our lives. It must literally permeate and course through everything we do.

Roles, work relationships, and reporting responsibilities must be modified. When you bring people together, you are setting the stage for a new idea. Each person is a wave of potential just waiting to be synergistically set off by an idea. In every idea there is a plethora of new ones just waiting to happen. In the past, the boss would walk by the water cooler to make sure people were not standing around and loafing. Today, managers should be walking by offices and asking why people are not standing around the water cooler and talking. Conversation is the name of the game.

In the past, the boss would walk by the water cooler to make sure people were not standing around and loafing. Today, managers should be walking by offices and asking why people are not standing around the water cooler and talking.

TIME/VALUE ADDED

Time is the currency of the nineties. Yes, we pay for products. But, increasingly, we pay for time. People value free time as much as they value wealth.

The goal is to find a niche. Telephone books are filled with business names that employ the words "quick", "jiffy", "instant", and "one-hour". Pizzas are now delivered in thirty minutes, and soon, with tracking telephones and ovens built right into the truck, they will deliver to your door in fifteen minutes. Jiffy Lube International, which offers a ten-minute oil change, has grown from nine outlets to over a thousand.

The nineties will be a decade in a hurry, an hour with only forty minutes. There will be only two kinds of workers: the fast and the fastest. The quick ones will realize that most of the efficiencies of the future will come from reducing distribution costs. Entrepreneurial niches will appear wherever distribution costs can be lowered or eliminated.

Price-based competition is now time based. Reputation based competition has become innovation based. Image is replaced by value, and all companies must be overlaid with great service and quality products.

At each step, individuals must ask over and over, "Is what I am doing adding value for the customer?" If not, why not? To manage the future we must add value. It is the only sure-fire way to sustain competitive advantage other than offering the lowest possible price. A few ideas:

- Be there first
- Develop programs and seminars for clients/customers
- Track and note client career achievements
- Identify the affluent and cater to their needs.
- Realize that extra small efforts can produce dramatic results
- Support a toll free number
- Implement faster turn-around
- Provide one-stop convenience
- Offer on-line information services such as an Internet World Wide Web home page

Everybody thinks you have to be a college graduate to succeed in the new economy. Not so. Education means "to bring out." Fortunately, there are millions of ways to do it.

I know window washers, lawn mowers, baby sitters, and house cleaners who make lots of money, love their jobs, and have found their niche, because they understand value added.

I am having my shoes shined in the Pittsburgh Airport and I watch a guy stuff five dollar bills in his pocket faster than you would believe.

He applies a gooey substance to my shoes, lights them on fire for a few seconds, and then hits them with a buff rag. Done. Shazam! It all happens in a minute. I have mirrors for shoes. It's the best shoe shine I have ever had in my life.

I give him my $5 bill—$3 for the shine, $2 for the tip and say, "I'm an economist and we often ask personal questions. Sir, how much money do you make shining shoes?"

He answers, "This year I should make about $50,000."

Shining shoes! Shining shoes!

But this is not just a shoe shine. This is a value added shoe shine.

I get out of an airplane in Atlanta and into a cab for a drive from the airport to a downtown hotel. The cab driver gives me a marvelous history lesson of Atlanta. He tells me about people, places, things, sports, and local companies—about everything. It is the best half hour I have ever spent in a cab.

The cab fare is seventeen dollars, plus a ten dollar tip. Handing him his money I say, "I feel a bit embarrassed.

You are terrific. Why, that cab ride is worth one hundred dollars."

He looks me right in the eye and replies, "Excuse me, sir, but a lot of my customers do tip me one hundred dollars."

I ask him my question. "I'm an economist and we often ask personal questions. Sir, how much money do you make driving a cab in Atlanta?"

With a grin from ear to ear he says, "Well, this year, just a little under $100,000." He pauses, and then adds, "tax free!"

We are not talking about a successful mid-level manager. We are talking about a cab driver. A cab driver!

I have shared this story with hundreds of cab drivers around the country and encouraged them to do the same thing. A number have written me to say it works. A value-added cab driver can easily double his daily receipts. When you exceed expectations, the sky's the limit.

For those of us in sales jobs, there are all kinds of opportunities to add value to what we do.

For the solid, steady, no complaint, no noise customer, the one we so easily take for granted, how about this note: "It is so easy to take for granted people like you. I just wanted to let you know I appreciate your business and the friendship we have established."

What about writing a note to the complaining customer: "Thank you for bringing your problem to my attention. I am working on a quick and satisfactory resolution."

There are also opportunities to firm up your relationship with new clients who place a second order or decide to up their level of business.

How about the customer who has called to thank you for the good job you've done for them? What a time for making deposits in their emotional bank account and thanking them.

Or, what about the client who has had a difficult time: divorce, illness, or a death in the family? Many people who buy from us would probably say "I don't care about how much you know until I know how much you care." This is the time to show that you do.

And best of all, what about a note to the good customer who can bring you new customers? Word of mouth is the best kind of selling. Going the extra mile is a privilege, not an obligation. It really pays.

Know your clients. Spend time listening to them. Get in their shoes. Respond in unique and creative ways. The race, after all, goes to those who know their customers best.

The access to people is through their concerns.

Service is not just *a* competitive edge, it is *the* competitive edge.

You must not just give lip service, you must give heart service.

Service cannot just be an afterthought; it must be *the* thought.

You tell people with your head but you sell them with your heart.

Never refuse to do the little things, for from the little things are built the big things.

When it comes to service, you can never stop thinking about it.

Good enough never is.

You have just read a few signs-of-the-times wall plaques exhorting us to greater service. Now, how do you do it? Does service have anything to do with being a servant? Are we short of service because we are short of servants?

SIX IDEAS FOR SERVING SUCCESSFULLY

Number One:

Does anyone remember the 1957 movie, "The Bridge on the River Kwai?" A prison-camp commander made the statement, "Be happy in your work."

Discover and develop your gifts. What do you like to do? What do you have to offer to others? What are your natural talents? Work is more fun than fun if you are doing what you want to do. If you have a job you love, you'll never work a day in your life.

So, begin by asking: What do I believe (and others substantiate) is my greatest contribution to the lives of other people?

Number Two:

As you discover and develop your gifts, pursue and develop relationships which give or will give you the chance to exercise your talent. When you're in the right job, you won't have to struggle to succeed.

Begin by asking: "Am I in a place of influence where I have the freedom to best serve people with what I have to offer?" If not, how do I get there?

Number Three:

Become an outward focused person. Stop contemplating your navel. Redirect the tendency to always think about yourself. Purge the tyranny of being self-serving to becoming "others-serving." Do not let the "urgents" in your life get in the way of the "importants." In today's business environment, everyone is in sales. Learn how to sell yourself and your ideas by being positive and optimistic, and by helping people reach their goals.

Number Four:

Demonstrate your actions by articulating a vision and plan that leads to your growth and that of others. Efforts and courage are not enough without purpose and dedication. Write it down. How? When? Who is the who that is going to do what by when? We all have the time to do the things we feel important.

Begin by asking: Am I involved in something that makes others successful?

Number Five:

Do what you say. Keep your promises. Doing the little things inevitably leads to big things. But note: there are no little things. As Walt Disney once said, "Always remember that the whole thing was started by a mouse." The difference between the ordinary and the extraordinary are the details. Small, insignificant little things are really the basis for bigger things.

Begin by asking, "What consistency is seen between what I say I am and what others see me to be?" Over the long run, it is the quality of our deeds and the style of our actions. Character is what counts. Reputation is what others say you are. Character is what you are. Many of us can be better than our reputations, but none of us can be better than our principles. Yes, we are what we habitually do. Excellence and keeping promises is not an art. It is a habit.

Number Six:

Aim to make others great. Begin by asking: "How can I make others successful?" Jesus, the greatest teacher in the world said, "I came not to be served, but to serve."

All of us can recognize and appreciate others. All of us can lift, exalt and encourage. Many of us can formulate greater challenges and responsibility for those with whom we work. And a few of us have the power to design enhanced financial rewards and provide more security for people and their families.

In closing, one of the biggest factors in success is the courage to undertake something. Not to act is to act. Not to decide is to decide. Even a mosquito doesn't wait for an opening—he makes one. Perfect aim is useless, unless you pull the trigger. Do something.

If you're not prepared then none of this makes a difference. But if you are prepared, you have to take a step of faith. Leap and the net will appear.

Enormous strides have been made in the last 15 years when businesses introduced total quality management, revamped incentive systems, empowered employees, decentralized, downsized, re-engineered, re-structured, outsourced, and partnered. Did they all work? Not always.

But the point is they did something. They kept what
worked and threw out what didn't.

We must do the same. Individuals in the contract
society must have a penchant for action—a willingness to
try new things. Thinking, considering, wishing, contemplating, deciding, and determining are all important. But
nothing has the power of action. In the words of Nike,
"Just Do It."

Chapter Seven

POLITICS VERSUS AMERICA'S SCHOOL CHILDREN

"If we think we can rely on education to change education" observed Wilbert Smith, former member of the Pasadena, California Unified School District Board of Education, "we have a rude awakening ahead of us." For more than a decade, in particular, since the publication in 1983 of *A Nation At Risk: The Imperative for Educational Reform*, hundreds of millions of taxpayer and foundation dollars have been devoted to studies concerned with improving the performance of the public school system.

The reasons are not difficult to understand. One 1985 study found that less than half of U.S. high school graduates could locate information in a news article or almanac. Barely 50 percent could follow travel directions on a map. Only about half knew how to enter deposits and checks and, in turn, balance a checkbook. Another study found that only about one third of seventeen-year-olds could place the Civil War in the right *half* century. In a science proficiency test, American ten-year-olds scored in the middle of a group of other industrial and developing economies; but fourteen-year-olds scored near the bottom and American eighteen-year-olds finished last.

"Is it possible that there is something inherent in America's traditional institutions of democratic governance that systematically creates and nurtures the kinds of schools that no one really wants?"

-John E. Chubb & Terry M. Moe

Education budgets continue to rise in real terms even though SAT scores fall or remain a good deal below those of thirty years ago. Remedial instruction remains a large and growing cost to America's colleges and universities. In 1989 through 1990, 30 percent of all college freshman enrolled in at least one remedial course. A 1990 survey of two hundred major U.S. corporations found that 22 percent must teach reading, 41 percent teach writing, and 31percent teach arithmetic to their employees. In 1990, one estimate suggested that American corporations were spending $25 billion annually providing basic skills to their workers. The costs of these large remedial expenditures by higher education and business need to be added to the totals of public school system budgets if we really want to know what the existing system is costing the American people.

In spite of the manifest failure of monopoly government school systems, education expert Myron Lieberman has observed an interesting implication of these monopoly conditions: "We come to a paradoxical conclusion . . . Public education has flourished because it fails to educate effectively." Throughout the past thirty years, falling SAT scores have been the justification for larger schools budgets. In fact, name a government bureaucracy that does *not* ask for more money when the job they are assigned is not being accomplished. Slower mail delivery requires larger postal service budgets. Higher crime rates lead to bigger requests for law enforcement expenditures. As government poverty programs expand, the incidence of poverty remains high. And in spite of hundreds of billions being spent, HUD and HHS claim the problem is not enough taxpayer money for the poor.

"If we can accept the fact that Communism can fall after seventy-some years, I do not see why we cannot stand and fight a bureaucracy [the public school monopoly] that is doing a terrible job, that is harming our children, and that is hurting this whole country."

-Polly Williams, Wisconsin legislator

Our schools are not in trouble because the U.S. is poor. We spend more money per student than any country in the world. Fifty percent of high school graduates are not prepared for entry level jobs—not because they are incapable. Most are as capable as any in the world. But rather, education is in trouble because the world has changed and education has not. American schools are fundamentally out of step with the larger social and economic realities of the Information Age and global economy that we have discussed in this book. How long do you think it would take a school system competing for students to figure out that their schools were under utilized? Or, that they should be open all year with longer hours, have extended day programs, supervised homework and enriched after school programs? Do you think students and parents might be attracted to such ideas?

But it will not happen as long as the National Education Association and its state and local affiliates, the nation's largest and most formidable labor union, retains its monopoly power. The liberal left politicking of the NEA is nowhere better seen than in the unproven feel-good programs that now infest our public school classrooms. Instead of emphasizing core academics, they have turned classrooms into "safe environments" where no student "fails" and where "fairness" is encouraged over excellence.

SPENDING MORE IS NOT THE ANSWER

"Give us more money and we will do a better job," administrators argue. Don't believe it. The evidence is overwhelming that education spending is not significantly correlated with student performance. Since 1986 the Kansas City school system has plowed incredible amounts of taxpayer money into new magnet schools, countless innovative educational programs, and the finest physical plant that money can buy. Through 1992, $1.3 billion had been spent in the district, over and above the normal school budget. This supplementary funding represented an extra $36,111 for each of the system's 36,000 students. As *The Economist* reported, "both in the scope of their programs and in the quality of their physical facilities, Kansas City's schools now match any in the world."

Unfortunately, the results of this experiment have been very disappointing. Through 1992, the vast expenditures of money brought no improvement at all to the children's scores in standardized tests of reading and math. Drop out rates have continued to rise.

"It's time to admit that public education operates like a planned economy, a bureaucratic system in which everybody's role is spelled out in advance and there are few incentives for innovation and productivity. It's no surprise that our school system does not improve. It more resembles the communist economy than our own market economy."

-Albert Shanker, President, AFT

Repeated claims by the educational establishment that more government spending is the answer, especially from their unions, the National Education Association (NEA) and the American Federation of Teachers (AFT), seem clearly wrong. It appears that something is inherently inefficient about the political provision of goods and services, including education. While the NEA and others in government schools frequently defend the existing system in the name of protecting the interests of the poor and disadvantaged, the Kansas City experiment, as well as others, clearly demonstrate that they are being poorly served.

BREAK THE MONOPOLY

The government school system needs a healthy dose of Tom Peters' *Liberation Management* in combination with an open-market environment in which private-for-profit schools would provide the necessary competition to government schools. The only force powerful enough to break the government's monopolistic hold on education is the pressure of competition. Hierarchical organizations that do not work very well in corporate America are forced by the competitive market process to change or go out of business. In contrast, the public bureaucracy has no equivalent discipline. No bottom line. No ownership.

Even important mainstream Democrats are seeing that centralization and bureaucracy are killing our children's hopes for a decent education. Here is how the Progressive Policy Institute, Clinton's main think tank, describes government schools:

> Our public school districts display in classic form the over centralization and bureaucratic rigidity that afflicts government in general. Their inability to adapt to new circumstances and to the public demand for improvement is rooted in the monopoly character of the system.

Monopolistic government school systems profoundly illustrate the implications of this distinction. No amount of marginal restructuring of the public school system—with, for example, magnet schools, school-based management, empowering teachers, performance based education, etc.—is going to help very much if the existing political structure of monopoly and bureaucratic control remains in place.

Public schools often look like communist models of society. All decisions are made from above. Both are fundamentally totalitarian, spending much energy to control people. Both view private property and profit-seeking as sources of conflict, alienation and problems. And both narrow the choices people have to one: one party, one point of view, one make of car, and for governmentalists, one choice of school.

GOVERNMENT COMPARED TO PRIVATE

Government and private school comparisons of efficiency and productivity are revealing. In 1991, the Los Angeles Unified School District had 810,000 students and 3,500 employees at administration headquarters. In contrast, the Catholic archdiocese in L.A. County had 100,000 students and just 25 central administrators. The *Los Angeles Times* reported that only half of each educational dollar reached the classroom in the Los Angeles public school system. At the time, 607 people in the L.A. Unified School District had salaries of $80,000 or more.[1]

Chicago offers another interesting comparison. In 1990, the government school system had 420,000 students and 1,600 administrators. The Catholic archdiocese in Chicago had 149,000 students, with only 39 central administrators. In short, the educational bureaucracy has mushroomed into a mighty glob of people parasitically sucking more money from the taxpayer while accomplishing less and less. No matter how badly they perform, they will not be put out of business.

Even large spending differentials among public schools don't buy either efficiency or productivity. For example, in New Jersey, where public education expenditures average approximately $7,571 per student per year, a child receives a $90,000 primary and secondary education from public funds. By contrast, in the state of Utah, where public education expenditures average approximately $2,571 per student per year, a child receives a $30,000 primary and secondary education from public funds. And yet, as unbelievable as it may seem, despite this vast 300 percent difference in cost, the average education received by a public school student in Utah is actually superior to that of a public school student in New Jersey. The high school graduation percentage in Utah is higher than it is in New Jersey (80.6 percent as opposed to 77.2 percent), and the composite average SAT scores for Utah are considerably higher than the composite average SAT scores for New Jersey (1034 contrasted to 893).

School organization is out of sync with the world today. As businesses increasingly realize that power must be diffused—that power must flow down and out; that hierarchical management styles no longer reflect today's reality—schools have marched in the other direction and become even larger.

In 1960, there were approximately 40,000 school districts. Today, there are fewer than 16,000 school districts. As the 1976 to 1986 enrollment in the Chicago public school declined by 18 percent and teachers fell by 8 percent, over that same period the number in public school administration grew by 47 percent.

In both Chicago and Los Angeles, per pupil costs are, at minimum, one-third lower in the Catholic schools than the government schools. Economist Robert Genetski, for example, conducted a study in which he adjusted public school costs downward to make allowances for students with mental disabilities and other factors, and adjusted the costs of the Catholic schools up, including an adjustment that would reflect paying salaries at levels comparable to those in the public schools. Even with the most liberal adjustments, private school costs were anywhere from 45 percent to 77 percent lower than in government schools.

With government production of education, bureaucrat and teacher interests are favored at the expense of parents and students. The 2.1 million members of the NEA, with an annual budget of more than $140 million, and the AFT's 780,000 members, with an annual budget of $55 million, repeatedly advocate policies that are in their own self interests. On such issues as aid to parents of children in private schools, child labor laws, duration of compulsory education, and minimum wage laws, the NEA takes a position that advances the welfare of teachers and/or their union.

District consolidation, rising school size and centralized funding have all served to weaken local control over schools, reducing the ability of parents and local taxpayers to control school policies.

In addition, large, tax financed public school districts become ripe targets for unions. In 1961, not one teacher had a collective bargaining unit. By 1991, over 80 percent of teachers were in a collective bargaining unit. And because they are unionized, firing an incompetent teacher is difficult. *Forbes Magazine* has recently noted that "the

NEA's rise is directly linked with the thirty year decline of American education."

But what do teachers in urban schools think of public schools? Don't ask what they *say,* but rather find out where they *send* their own kids. Studies indicate that twenty to 50 percent of the children of public school teachers attend private schools.

"In essence the public school is America's collective farm. Innovation and productivity are lacking in American education for basically the reasons they are scarce in Soviet agriculture: absence of competition and market forces.

-Lewis J. Perelman, Author

Again, the problem is the politically controlled nature of the system and not the individual teachers or administrators. It is not an issue of bad versus good people. Of course teachers look out for their own interests. We all do. But the structure of incentives in a tax financed, government bureaucracy guarantees perverse outcomes. "There is no way whatsoever of doing something about this problem," according to Nobel laureate Milton Friedman, "except by introducing competition, by enabling customers, parents and children, to have alternatives among which they can choose."

CHOICE

The pat answer is "choice." But, the concept of parental choice has about as many meanings as there are interested parties. Even the education establishment talks about choice in schools, as long as parents and students are only permitted to choose from traditional government schools and their survival and budgetary support remains guaranteed. Indeed, teachers' unions have offered advocates of serious reform token choice (for example, the Milwaukee experiment that applies to the minuscule portion of the school system's students) in order to deflect demands for a thorough-going competitive system.

"Choice will destroy public schools, leave the poor behind, and might be unconstitutional to boot."

- President Bill Clinton

Choice plans that do not free up the supply side of the market place, that is, plans that fail to offer real alternative education models from which to choose—public schools, non-profit schools *and* private-for-profit schools—will never bring the benefits of competitive rivalry. An analogy would be a situation in which government food stamps could only be spent in government grocery stores. A politically driven system in which schools are not allowed to emerge spontaneously in response to what parents and students want precludes educational reform.

The only way the parasitic infestation of monopoly government schools can be cured is to sever the parasite at its point of attachment. Let parents take their money where they believe they get the most benefit. We do it for everything else, why not schools?

A truly open market, that is, an absence of legal barriers to entering the schooling business, would break the back of the existing monopoly political control.

A competitive situation, in contrast, would find a principal who has chosen to be at that school and has chosen the school's educational program and faculty. Each teacher, of course, would have chosen to work at that particular school. And each student has chosen to study at that particular school. Everyone involved in the enterprise has "bought into" such a school. Parents, teachers and students would be transformed from captives into consumers.

In many public schools, however, the principal is assigned to the school, the curriculum is determined in detail by the central bureaucracy, the teachers are assigned, and the students are required to attend. Nobody has bought in. Nobody has made a choice. Every aspect of the school is dictated from above.

John Chubb and Terry Moe in *Politics, Markets and America's Schools* show that school organization matters for student performance and that autonomy has the "strongest influence on the overall quality of school organization." They observe that in a market system the authority to make educational choices is radically decentralized to those most immediately involved.

Schools controlled only by the market are free to organize any way they want. An environment of competition and choice gives them a strong incentive to move toward the kinds of "effective-school" organizations that academics and reformers would like to impose on public schools.

Chubb and Moe also found that school organization is most importantly determined by whether a school is in the private sector or the government sector. Independence prevails in private schools.

Myron Lieberman in his book *Public Education: An Autopsy,* captures an important idea. In designing the rules under which a truly open and competitive education system would operate, one that would offer real choice to parents and their children, "public authority must be put to use in creating a system that is almost entirely beyond the reach of public authority."

The advantages of a competitive system are numerous. In a competitive market system of public schools and non-profit and proprietary private schools, for-profit private schools in particular would have a strong incentive to define and measure standards of comparison and performance. The motivation? Survival. Currently, government schools have a strong interest in avoiding measurable comparisons of performance. No comparisons, no accountability.

The defenders of the status quo argue that controversial views would be presented in a biased fashion by private schools. In fact, government schools and their supporters, namely the NEA and the AFT, are already biased in favor of blessing the political solutions, as they are direct beneficiaries of government largess at the expense of the taxpayer. One need only review the official position of the NEA on racial quotas, tax policy, labor unions, environmental issues and any number of other policy issues to realize the liberal bias of educational interest groups. It is illustrative that of the 4,928 delegates to the 1992 Democratic National Convention, 512 were NEA or AFT members, representing the largest interest group among the delegates. William Bennett, the former secretary of education under Ronald Reagan, has called the NEA "the absolute heart and center of the Democratic Party."

One of the oldest and most misleading rhetorical arguments for government education is that it is essential to representative government. But, in fact, the U.S. Constitution and American democracy were in place and thriving almost a century before public schools came to be the dominant system of education in the United States. The benefits of government schools, it turns out, served largely to discriminate against and domesticate the catholic immigrants that came to the U.S., especially during and after the 1840s.

President Clinton's Goals 2000: Educate America Act is largely cosmetic. But happily for government educators and monopolists, it will continue to pump more taxpayer money into the system because its performance is so poor. The administration preaches national delivery standards, which means that the government school systems, as is the practice of the Department of Defense and the U.S. Postal Service, extend the practice of using their spending as the measure of their performance.

Goals 2000 increases the centralization of primary and secondary education in America, which means more bureaucracy, not less. The federal government will, as Representative Jack Reed of Rhode Island said, "compel states to fix failing schools." But the Clintons know better than to trust the bureaucratic government system. Supposedly staunch supporters of the public school system, the Clintons are sending their daughter Chelsea to Sidwell Friends School, a prestigious private academy in Washington, D.C. "As parents, we believe this decision is best for our daughter at this time in her life based on our changing circumstances," says the President. But they have the means to choose. The poor generally do not.

The contradictions in the current government system are far too numerous to ignore. As Myron Lieberman has observed, "the pro-market forces will have one ineradicable advantage in the years ahead. That advantage is the inherent futility of conventional school reform."

DO SCHOOLS MATTER?

Why does it matter that our schools succeed? There are two main reasons. One is that students who are unsuccessful in school are less productive. Those kids who use their public school education as a way out of poverty are in real trouble, inevitably ending up with unskilled jobs.

Increasing competition from foreign producers in our low-skill industries has hit the badly educated even harder. Cornell University economist John H. Bishop, in his path breaking article in the March 1989 *American Economic Review*, presented estimates suggesting that since test scores began declining in 1967, the U.S. Gross National Product (GNP) was $87 billion lower in 1987 than it would have been had our education system been doing its job properly. He estimated the present value of this loss at about $3.2 trillion, which is approximately three-quarters of the 1987 GNP. The loss in income, in 1987 dollars, was about $13,000 per person.[2]

A second reason we need our schools to succeed is just as important as the first. If our schools fail, kids will never understand the delights of learning and understanding. Their self-esteem, personal growth, and opportunity for advancement are all linked to a good education.

So, while we wait for choice to work its way through the ballot box and the legislature, there is something you can do now. There is a privatization effort that seeks to recover the rights and responsibilities of individuals as citizens.

In 1991, Patrick Rooney, chairman of the board of the Golden Rule Insurance Company in Indianapolis, began the Educational CHOICE Charitable Trust program. Basically, this program gives tuition grants to low-income families in Indianapolis. While critics of choice argue the poor will be left behind, Rooney argues that large numbers of public schools today are exclusive, segregated, and unequal. The "haves" choose a private school for their children or buy a home in the right neighborhood. The "have-nots" are trapped. Choice gives the "have-nots" the same opportunity as the "haves." Rooney emphasizes that the grants, which are made to elementary school students, cover half the annual tuition, up to a maximum grant of $800. To be eligible, parents must live in the boundaries of the Indianapolis public school district and must have a family income below the income that makes them eligible for the federal school lunch program. Half the funds are allocated to families that are enrolling their children in private schools for the first time, and the other half are given to families whose children have already been enrolled in private school. In the first year of the program, 1991-1992, 744 children enrolled at fifty-eight private Indianapolis schools. Two hundred and forty-seven families were on the waiting list. Twenty-seven percent of families that participated had family incomes below $10,000, and 89 percent had family incomes below $25,000.[3]

While the public school establishment asserts that choice would create an inequitable elitist educational system, Rooney's experience is that a market-driven educational system will, in fact, spur improvements in the way schools operate. Capitalism works everywhere it is tried. Why not schools?

Educational trust choice programs are springing up everywhere. Pat Rooney told me that questionnaires from the parents participating in the Indianapolis Choice Program indicate their main concerns are values, then safety, and third, education. When given a choice, most parents prefer schools that teach strong Christian/Judaeo principles. Are you surprised?

Harvard economist Richard Freeman's recent study discovered that inner-city youth with a strong religious orientation have a 47 percent lower high school dropout rate, are 54 percent less likely to use drugs and commit 50 percent less crime. The evidence is everywhere. It is not coincidental that the breakdown of family and religious values has coincided with increases in crime, drug abuse, and homelessness.

What is the solution to our failing public school system? The solution is a school system that emphasizes hard work, educational basics, values and personal responsibility. Since each parent will differ in exactly what they want for their kids, however, choice is imperative. The issue is not public versus private. It is choice versus lack of choice; between voluntary association and legal coercion. Americans have long experienced the variety of goods and services that spring from competition and the private sector. Every poll shows that Americans are ready to support the concept of school choice.

Every time you get a chance to vote against a bond issue or a school tax increase, do it. The only way we will take back control of our schools is by cutting the monopolist's allowance.

If you are interested in starting an educational trust voucher program for your city, please call 1-317-293-7600.

Chapter Eight

TEA TIME ON THE POTOMAC

U.S. Highway 98 turns east out of Fairhope, a little town of 7,000 people in deep southwest Alabama, and winds through new-growth pine forests where cotton once ruled. At the second road past a narrow bridge, there stands a tree. The first time I saw it was in the summer of 1990. In my opinion, it was the most exquisite, picturesque tree in America.

This Southern Live Oak was a tree of unbelievable beauty. Five hundred years old, just a sapling when Christopher Columbus landed in America, it was over 65 feet tall, has a trunk circumference of 27 feet, and a spread of 150 feet from tip to tip. The American Forestry Association keeps a National Register of big trees. This one would probably be at the top of the list.

Twice as old as our country, it had been hit by lightning strikes hundreds of times, had endured dozens of hurricanes, had withstood more rain storms than you could count, and had taken on wind, insect infestation, disease, drought, flood, blistering sun, and just about everything else. But, there it stood—hundreds of tons of tree— beautiful, magnificent, breath taking . . . until . . .

Until a fateful night in October when a man with a chain saw banded the tree, stripping it of its bark and its lifeblood.

Immediately, experts were called in. On October 16, 1990 the initial grafting was begun. One hundred and thirty-eight small bridge grafts and 65 large ones were grafted from 5 living trees. A 140 foot well was dug to provide water to the sprinkler heads mounted atop a telephone pole some 65 feet in the air. The sprinkler poured water over the entire crown of the tree every ten minutes during each daylight hour. An intensive care apparatus was rigged around the trunk of the tree to control inside temperature at 80 degrees and maintain a relative humidity of between 90 and 100 percent. Twenty-four hour surveillance of the tree was maintained. Tens of thousands of dollars were collected to do anything and everything to save this national monument.

The efforts were in vain. The tree died.

Capitalism in America can be likened to that tree. Professors have denounced it. Writers have mocked it. Scholars have criticized it. Governments have taxed, regulated, and done everything they could to kill it. Socialists said it would collapse. Clergy call it greedy. Liberals call it unfair. It's demise has been predicted, prophesied and forecast.

Even its supporters are concerned that capitalism won't survive. Government is so big, so powerful, and so intrusive they write, that entrepreneurs will not be able to survive its onslaught.

But, freedom's defenders are fighting back.

William Simon wrote a best selling book entitled, *A Time for Truth*. Holding the office of Secretary of the Treasury under President Gerald Ford, he said the following in one of his numerous congressional testimonies:

> The real issue (our problem in America) is the government's share of the Gross National Product—of the earnings of every productive citizen in this land. That is the issue on which we should concentrate. What does it mean for the American dream? What does it mean for our way of life? What does it mean for our free enterprise system? What is our free enterprise system? Isn't free enterprise related to human freedom, to political and social freedom? When the government absorbs the GNP to the levels that we have seen the very cohesion of civilized society is destroyed. That is the road we are on today. That is the direction in which the "humanitarians" are leading us. But there is nothing "humanitarian" about the collapse of a great industrial civilization. There is nothing "humanitarian" about the panic, the chaos, the riots, the starvation, the deaths that will ensue. There is nothing "humanitarian" about the dictatorship that must inevitably take over as terrified people cry out for leadership. There is nothing "humanitarian" about the loss of freedom. That is why we must be concerned about the cancerous growth of government and its steady devouring of our citizens' productive energies. That is why we must be concerned about deficits and balancing the budget. The issue is not bookkeeping. It is not accounting. The issue is the liberty of the American people.

Martin Gross, the former editor of Book Digest and experienced reporter who covered Washington, D.C. for dozens of years, wrote a book called *The Government Racket: Washington Waste From A To Z*.

> People are suspicious that something is *fundamentally* wrong in Washington. And they are right. Hundreds of billions of dollars are being taken from them each year under false pretenses. In fact, waste of enormous proportions is built into the federal system, though most of it is expertly hidden. Waste is more prevalent than efficiency; more common than good works. If it continues at its present pace, not only will it bankrupt the nation fiscally, it will destroy us morally as well. Government is a failure, a fallacy, a myth, and a racket.

Recent studies show the Washington, D.C. area as having seven of the ten richest jurisdictions in all of America. Falls Church, Alexandria, Arlington, and Fairfax County, all in Virginia and all bedroom communities of Washington, have no manufacturing, no seaport, no financial services and little industry that anyone would call productive. Yet, they are fabulously richer than almost any place in the United States. They produce legislation, laws, regulations, and a war on poverty that has failed everywhere but in Washington, D.C.

James T. Bennett, an Eminent Scholar at George Mason University holds the William P. Snavely Chair of Political Economy and Public Policy, and Thomas J. DiLorenzo, a Professor of Economics in the Sellinzer School of Business and Management at Loyola College, co-authored a book called *Official Lies*. It is a non-partisan look at the many ways in which politicians and bureaucrats use propaganda to manipulate the machinery of government and advance their own interests. It is a compelling indictment of how Washington bureaucrats take money from taxpayers and use it to buy their votes. Most Americans do not appreciate how much of the government's power actually springs from its control of information. Bennett and DiLorenzo's book reveals how our rulers routinely twist and trample the truth.

Official Lies opens the curtain on our modern wizard of Oz: the vast propaganda machine headquartered in Washington, D.C. "From welfare to drugs to everything, Uncle Sam consistently misrepresents problems so that his muscles can grow ever larger. Poverty statistics have been systematically overblown in order to win greater spending on social programs. Astonishingly, 22,000 households officially designated as "poor" own Jacuzzis or heated swimming pools."

You name it. Government will spend your money on it.

Six million to the National Seafood Council; $500,000 to study the effects of cigarette smoking on dogs; $13 million to repair a privately owned dam in South Carolina; $500,000 for the 1992 America Flora Exposition; $49 million for a rock and roll museum; $66,000 to determine the average length of a flight attendant's nose (2.8 inches); $942,000 for fishing gear entanglement research; $375,000 to renovate the House beauty parlor; $8 million for Senate elevators; $2 million to renovate the House restaurant; $98 million for Congressional franked mail, and on and on. Add it all up, $1.5 trillion of government spending.

Polls now find that 75 percent of Americans think the country needs to make changes in the way the Federal Government works; 73 percent of all Americans believe the Federal Government creates more problems than it solves; and 63 percent believe the government is "primarily an adversary in their lives."

Fortunately, freedom's future will not be determined by liberal writers, socialist professors, governmental activists, benevolent do-gooders, or the aggregate statistical abstractions of interventionist economists. Rather, it will be the wisdom of informed people who are determined to slay the leviathan. The November 8, 1994 election was just the beginning.

The Information Revolution described in Chapter Two and restated here, as well as the forces discussed in this chapter, will soon reduce government to a size that would have made Jefferson proud. Let's look at the reasons.

THE DECENTRALIZATION OF INFORMATION AND POWER

In times past, when Americans built something, they would organize, congregate, roll up their sleeves, and make it happen. They would get together as communities, families, churches, or whatever to get the job done. But to do so, they had to give up doing it alone. A degree of personal freedom was sacrificed to achieve the greater good of corporate accomplishment.

Naturally, people in community felt a need to appoint a leader. Bishops, kings, and presidents were anointed, picked, or democratically chosen. Over time, the rulers would assemble in an executive suite, a White House, a capitol building, or some other kind of palace structure fit for an elite.

Information, of course, only traveled one way—from the rulers to the ruled. Top down. Command and control. They had the information. They had the power.

People put up with this, of course, because the gains of living in the city or under an authority outweighed living in the wilderness under anarchy. Strength of numbers and unity allowed this structure to continue. There was nothing out there that could challenge it.

Given the technology of Madison's time and even up to 1980, it all made sense. We would elect a representative government to vote for us, empower our officials way beyond what we deemed necessary, and hope that government would somehow control itself.

It didn't. It won't. It never will.

James Madison, among others, was not unaware of the problems associated with the granting of coercive power to government and the fragile character of human freedom:

> But what is government, but the greatest of all reflections on human nature? If men were angels, no government would be necessary. If angels were to govern men neither external nor internal controls on government would be necessary. In framing a government, which is to be administered by men, the great difficulty lies in this: You must first enable the government to control the governed; and in the next place, oblige it to control itself.

Fortunately, however, the world is moving from a technology of control to a technology of freedom. Just as the mainframe computer was broken apart and made into hundreds of desktop machines, so has the large, central telephone exchange been replaced by distributed switches with multiple levels of inter-connection between them. In other words, centralism has given way to dispersion and empowerment.

It is a Digital Revolution that will transform our government, our community, our businesses, and our lives. Networks are being connected to networks— television networks; radio networks; conventional phone networks; cellular phone networks; video and home entertainment networks; data transport networks; wireless networks. Not to mention CNN; C-SPAN; Internet, CompuServe, Compustat, Globalvantage, interactive video; telecomputers; fax machines and photo copiers; all interlinked, all interconnected, and all empowering people.

What happens when everybody has access to voluminous amounts of information? What happens when people everywhere are brought together by networks that defy the imagination? What happens when people themselves have the information necessary to vote for themselves? Do they want government to make choices for them?

As the telecommunication network becomes reality, community can be formed anywhere and everywhere. Place doesn't matter. Neither does distance. Everybody is informed. Everybody is connected. Individual to individual. Point to point. The buyers and sellers of the world are brought together in the same way that every road in the country leads to your front door. And, importantly, government's role and control in all of this will be perilously close to zero.

Again, of all the forces eating away at big government, perhaps the most persistent is the flow of information—information that governments previously monopolized, cooking it up as they saw fit and redistributing it the way they wanted. Their monopoly of knowledge about things happening around the world enabled them to fool and control the people, because only they possessed real facts in anything like real time.

Elected officials and bureaucrats obscure and distort inconvenient facts, fantasize bogus crisis and constantly propagandize the citizenry to achieve their own ends. Ninety percent of a politician's job is to manipulate the machinery of government to advance the states' interests.

---

*Ninety percent of a politician's job
is to manipulate the machinery of government to
advance the states' interests.*

There was a time when we thought we couldn't throw the rascals out. After all, they had bolted the door, put sand bags at the gates, and had all the artillery of tax monies at hand to shoot down any of the dissenting barbarians. They had large staffs. They had the franking privilege. And they had the chutzpah and chicanery to use the power of incumbency. A French poet once said that "politics is the art of preventing people from taking part in affairs which properly concern them."

Today, of course, people everywhere are able to get the information they want directly from all corners of the world. Everyone can watch CNN. Televising congressional actions twenty four hours a day on C-SPAN is an on-going commercial for term limits. Every show should open with the caption:

They stack it thick in Congress,
it's really kind of raw.
What should be spread by tractor,
they enact and call it law.

Fax machines spread information like wildfire. Telephone calls now number 100 million an hour and that number will soon double.

Technology is on the side of liberty. The fiber-optic, multi-media electronic network means that more and more people will have more and more information and it will be available immediately. C-SPAN television is the Ford Model T of direct democracy. Direct referenda conducted by everyone pushing a button is only a few years away. Soon, we will be a free market democracy rather than a representative one. Modern networks will enable each of us to participate in political life. Politicians will be redundant, as every individual will vote on the issues they deem relevant. The development of on-line political activism will expose power-grabbing politicians for what they are. We will have governance without government, as effective community minded consensus emerges from the millions of daily interactions on Internet. Our ability to communicate views to elected representatives, if there are any, will be instantaneous. Term limits will insure we have citizen legislators for a specific time and not a lifetime.

Most politicians campaign against Washington as if it were a cesspool. But for the anointed and the elite, it becomes a hot tub. Perks, power, money, and status are just a few of the favors conveyed on our privileged leaders. They campaign as fiscal conservatives and then, when comfortably protected by distance and D.C., vote pork barrel politics with reckless abandonment. Conservative at home, liberal in Washington, like drunkards shouting of intemperance between cocktails, there is no problem that could not be helped by spending someone else's money. But the heat turns up as Americans tune in.

Look at talk radio as an example. There are currently more than 1,000 talk radio shows, up from just a few hundred a few years ago. Very much like the print media, the radio frequency spectrum, with a good dose of deregulation, now offers a very large number of alternative forums. Rush Limbaugh illustrates the possibilities. It is said that he is heard on 650 radio stations with a combined listening audience of 20 million people during a week's programming.

For three hours every day, this comic conservative of the airwaves provokes thought, provides entertainment, and drives governmentalists nuts. The White House monitors his show closer than they do Russia. His war on political correctness has people laughing from sea to shining sea.

In particular, a personality who does not follow the politically correct dogma of the liberal bias—that is favored by most large newspapers and the television networks—opens the debate to those who believe that their views are being ignored. The growth in the number and type of talk radio broadcasts strengthens public debate and insures a broader spectrum of views are heard.

New technologies will increase the channels and avenues by which individuals can become empowered to challenge old political ways of doing government's business. Perhaps the most important reason for the tidal change in the 1994 election was talk radio. Little did Ronald Reagan realize that when he rescinded the Fairness Doctrine on August 4, 1987, he was paving the way for a political revolution.

This opposition media has brought great consternation and angst to the big-government liberals in the Congress and to the Clinton Administration in particular. But things will only get worse for the entrenched, career politician. Issues will no longer be hidden from citizens by the politicians making deals in the proverbial smoky back room.

George Orwell was wrong in his book *1984*. It won't be Big Brother watching the people. It will be the people watching Big Brother. The more we know, the quicker we act. Tea Time is coming. In fact, it has already begun.

GOVERNMENT IS BROKEN

Government isn't working. Here's why.

Big government did not happen because evil people had evil intentions. Quite the contrary, it happened because there were a lot of good people who had good intentions. Opera houses, tennis courts, public buildings, food stamps, welfare checks, and free health care are all well intended social programs. Nobel laureate Milton Friedman for forty years has pounded away at the major flaws of the process.

First, people are doing good with other people's money. There is no end to the good that do-gooders will do with other people's money.

Second, you never spend someone else's money as carefully as you spend your own. Waste is inevitable.

And third, you cannot do good with another's money until you get it. So government must send a tax collector or a policeman to take your money away from you. Taking money requires force. Force is the fundamental requirement of the welfare state.

Doing good with other people's money and using force to get it predictably leads to disastrous results.

In the beginning it was easy. You have a lot of people paying taxes and a small number for whom you are trying to do good. Take a little from the many and give to the relatively few. Politics works best when you localize benefits and diffuse costs. You only have to steal a few dollars from everybody to subsidize the special interests you want to help. Those who pay the bill hardly notice. What's a few dollars, after all?

But the game gets tougher. As the number of people on the receiving end grows, you have to tax more and more, until you end up taxing 50 percent of the people to help 50 percent of the people. Early on, you take one dollar away from each of fifty people and give the fifty dollars to a needy person. A dollar does not ruffle anyone's feathers. But in the latter stages of the welfare state, the number of taxpayers falls because they rationally choose to be receivers, rather than payers. In turn, those taxed become more obstinate because the amounts needed from them is now much larger.

Witness the Beltway Bandits as they encircle Washington, D.C. and take aim at one-fourth of the nation's wealth. Washington has become a whorehouse. Electing a new piano player every four years doesn't seem to have much of an effect. Same song. New verse. The joke is on you. The yoke is on you. The yolk is on you.

H. L. Mencken once remarked than an election is just an advanced auction on stolen goods.

But what happens when Atlas Shrugs? What happens when good intentions produce bad results? What happens when doing good with other people's money backfires? What happens when working Americans get fed up? What happens when the government racket is exposed? What happens when their propaganda and official lies are regularly broadcast? Is it a time for truth? Or is it tea time, again?

America knows government doesn't work. Four trillion dollars since 1960 in social welfare spending to fight poverty has all been for naught. The incidence of poverty is as high or higher than it was thirty-five years ago. But now we also have an illegitimacy rate of about 30 percent (more than 60 percent among blacks in the large cities) as compared to roughly 5 percent in 1960. Senator Patrick Moynihan's warning in the late 1960s of the potential for a large dependent "underclass" has sadly, but predictably, come to pass.

The American people are coming to realize that government failure is pathological and not simply a matter of "reinventing government." In the summer of 1994, on ABC's "Night Line" program, the host, Ted Koppel, looked at his guest Vice President Al Gore and told him that his much ballyhooed reinventing government campaign of 1993 had come to nothing and deserved no better than a letter grade "D." The conclusion was confirmed by a Brookings Institute study published about the same time.

Reinventing government is not going to work because government is the wrong mechanism to give people what they want. The information economy demands agility and the efficiency of market signals which government does not possess. The speed that Wal-Mart shows in responding to consumer preferences is simply not possible for the U.S. Postal Service or the government run monopolistic school system.

If Marriott believes it must contract out the hotel's parking, then what are the implications for municipally operated parking garages? As GM, Sears, IBM, Apple, GE, the Union Pacific, and EDS restructure and cut whole levels of bureaucratic waste in order to serve their customers and, therefore, survive in this new age of technology, what are the odds that the EPA, FDA, Department of Agriculture, and the Department of Energy will do the same?

The University of Michigan released a study in late 1994 which involved an extensive consumer survey measuring consumer satisfaction. Over 46,000 people were asked how they felt about products and services provided by 200 companies and governmental agencies. Private sector, manufactured, non-durable goods, such as food, cigarettes, newspapers, and clothes scored highest with an average of 81.6 on a scale of 100. As you may have anticipated, public services such as the IRS and U.S.

Postal Service scored at the very bottom. In fact, the IRS was the lowest scorer with a pathetic score of only fifty-five. Are you surprised?

Government will never deliver efficient service. They do not have the price signals of profit and loss to tell them how to respond intelligently. Government people are not risking their own money. They have few incentives to be efficient or deliver good service with a smile. When you think monopoly, think government.

Government does not just waste money. Government is a waste of money. The issue is not for government to become efficient. The issue is whether to leave certain activities in the hands of government. To improve the performance of government is an exercise of superficial tinkering. The problem is not one of making it work better but rather to stop pretending it should be involved at all. As my friend John Fund of the *Wall Street Journal* has said, "If government were a consumer product on a store shelf it would be removed for being defective and sued for false advertising."

An apocryphal story: The number of farmers in the nation may be dropping dramatically, but the number of employees in the Department of Agriculture keeps rising. The story is told of a tour group in Washington visiting the Department of Agriculture and asking why one of the employees was sitting at his desk crying. The answer: "His farmer died."

PRIVATIZATION WORKS

Government will be engineered out of a job. The private sector works twenty-four hours a day to become more efficient. The efficiency gap between government provision and private provision has become too wide to ignore. All the things government previously attempted will be privatized because entrepreneurs can do them faster, better and cheaper. There are many reasons.

There is a fundamental distinction between the political means and the market means. The market means, which is to say the competitive market process, is characterized by a selective access to goods and services. That is, if an individual wishes to have a pair of shoes or see a movie, the person must provide something in exchange. In contrast, when goods or services are provided by government, equal access is usually guaranteed. The direct, out-of-pocket cost of using municipal tennis courts, public libraries, highways, neighborhood police patrols, or the city park, is zero. The good or service is provided "free" to all comers, and the cost is covered by the taxpayer. Those who use the service seldom have to pay, and those who pay often do not use. No attempt is made to match benefits and costs. This game has to fail. Everyone wants to get. Nobody wants to pay. In the case of the market place, however, the benefits of a new stereo album or a new coat are tied directly to a purchase price or the potential consumer is excluded from the enjoyment of that good.

Another problem is that political solutions often bring out the worst in people. When four people sit down to dine, for example, each will choose to suit their tastes. But, if the group has to "vote" on their selection of wine, they are confronted with a political problem. The person who insists on getting their way might have to use persuasion, coercion, their fists, or they might even resort to name calling, mud slinging, and telling others at the table how ugly they are. Leaving decisions to the market has all kinds of benefits, including the outcome of peaceful solutions.

Providing something for "free" has yet another important implication and, therefore, another reason for the demise of government provision. Inevitably, it means cross-subsidization. Those who use the city parks or the municipal transit system are subsidized by those who pay their local taxes but use and financially support a private park or drive their automobile to work. The gross mismatching of consumer benefits and tax costs in these situations generates both an efficiency and equity argument in favor of a system in which those who benefit from a service should be those who pay for it. The fundamental issue, after all, is freedom of choice. Individuals must be permitted to choose the services they want and, therefore, determine the ways they wish to spend their money.

Leaving decisions in the market has all kinds of benefits, including the outcome of peaceful solutions.

An unfortunate limitation in providing things for "free" is the false economic information given to the elected officials concerning the intensity of demand for municipal services. The function of price is to ration goods, services and resources. Most people would prefer to drive a Mercedes until they see its sticker price. A $50,000 price tag convinces them a Ford or Honda will do. Price not only measures the cost of acquisition, but it also indicates the intensity of demand. Goods and services provided "free" encourage wasteful consumption. Grocers would hardly be astounded to see their shelves emptied quickly if food prices were zero. Yet, government officials are quick to ask for larger budgets, whether for bridges, highways, education, tennis courts, or whatever, citing the intense demand, or need for the good or service in question. Providing things "free" only encourages people to want more.

But the house of cards is collapsing. Government is not a god. It does not create miracles. Government must tax before it can give. It is not a perpetual motion machine. The incentive to be a tax taker has finally overwhelmed the incentive to be a tax payer. Political solutions have failed because they are inefficient and unfair. Market solutions will be tried because they work.

Now don't get me wrong. I'm not saying the market is perfect. Far from it. Over the years the market has produced as many scoundrels, liars, and fakes as government. But the difference is this. When the market produces a lemon, I don't have to buy it. But, when government produces a dud, and that includes about everything they do, I have to pay anyway. If the market produces an Edsel, forget it. If, however, the government produces the welfare state, or federally funded abortions, or the license plate bureau, or government schooling, and the list is long—no choice buddy. Pay your money or go to jail.

Government cannot do anything *for* you that it did not do *to* you first. You've heard it before, but let me refresh your memory. The three biggest lies are (1) "your check is in the mail," (2) "I'll respect you in the morning," and (3) "I'm from the Federal Government and I'm here to help you."

Will government always provide schooling? No, we have already discussed its eminent collapse. Choice, vouchers and the competivization of schooling will break the government monopoly. And with telecommunications, an entire school or even a great library will one day reside on the student's desk in their computer.

Government operated prisons? They will be privatized and run efficiently.

Public roads and bridges? Those who use will pay. The private sector will run them.

Government lighthouses? The idea is antiquated. With advanced communications, ships can be tracked and guided privately. Every boat will have its own "lighthouse."

Railroads? Government, get out. Already, government has cost the taxpayer $9 billion. Amtrak? It would have been cheaper to buy an economy ticket on a commercial airline for the people who ride these trains then to continue the Amtrak boondoggle. Jay Leno, host of the Tonight Show, has been chiding Amtrak for its safety record for years. He's introduced an actor covered with bandages as the Amtrak president; has shown what he calls "Amtrak footage," a clip from an old black-and-white movie showing two steam engine trains exploding in a head-on collision; and recently has said "Amtrak could eliminate 600 jobs, not by firing employees but by sending them on a train trip."

Airports? Privatize them. Great Britain, Burbank in California, Westchester County in New York, and many,

many more are lightening the tax burdens of their citizens, lowering the costs of operation and are turning airports into a profitable operation.

Air traffic control? Most observers would argue that air traffic control would be both cheaper and probably safer if private, profit making operators were in charge. The average cost of operating and maintaining a Level I Tower (the lowest FAA rating in terms of volume of traffic) is three times as high for government towers as it is for private ones.

Fire departments? Rural/Metro Corporation is the private fire department that serves my hometown of Scottsdale, Arizona. In the twelve month period from September 1, 1993 to September 1, 1994, not a single person has died because of fire. For a city of 150,000 people, that is a tremendous feat. Although the number of fires has climbed in that twelve month period by 10 percent from 742 to 829, the total damage from those fires has been cut by about two-thirds, from $2.4 million to $754,000.

The main reasons? Rural/Metro pushes for fire prevention with a special attention on making every home safe from fire. In addition, private fire fighters use four inch fire hoses instead of the standard two and one-half inch hoses used by most government operated fire departments. It is amazing how much more water you can get on a fire with a bigger hose!

More government ownership? Many cities own airports, hospitals, golf courses, museums, and even classical music radio stations. They subsidize education, real estate, day care centers, and dozens of different businesses. But, they can't keep their streets clean, provide adequate police protection, and teach children how to read. Government is doing what they shouldn't do and not doing what they should be doing. Nothing is less productive than to make more efficient that which should not be done at all. Government has grown beyond its means. Streamlining services that government should not be doing is a waste of time and money. Privatization will eventually include everything, including money.

Money, you say? Yes, money has always been the province of government: they print it, control it, manage it, supply it, dispose of it, debauch it and devalue it.

Does money really have to be controlled by government? Money is really only what the market says it is. It is a convenient way to keep our wealth in small packages. Money has value because there are goods and services standing behind it. The value of money stands on trust and promises. In the past, it was the trust and promise of the government and central bank. Many times that trust was worthless.

But now we have in circulation thousands of private currencies, and the telecommunications age will only multiply them. Frequent flyer miles, trading stamps, credit card accounts, stocks, bonds—all these and many more have become "money." Money is being privatized, and when that happens government loses its vast power to tax and control.

THE GLOBAL ECONOMY

Globalization significantly reduces the power of government.

Politicians refuse to acknowledge that free enterprise requires economic growth as a pre-condition and that government requires economic contraction as a pre-condition. People want growth. They have increasingly realized that government has become the major obstacle for them to have the best and the cheapest from anywhere in the world. Putting tariffs on goods crossing borders is like having bandits lie in wait for the stage coach. It is robbery. And it is ridiculous. The idea of imposing tariffs on trade to assure freedom of competition is like breaking a man's leg to make him run faster.

The global economy is now producing wealth on a never before happened scale because governments are privatizing, lowering taxes and being relegated and ridiculed to their limited and proper place. Trade is not about warfare. Mutual gains from voluntary exchange is win/win. People want higher standards of living and government gets in the way.

With each passing day, it becomes harder and harder for politicians to unscramble the emerging global economy and reassert their declining power. The global economy is dissolving and reforming industry faster than government can regulate them.

Interestingly, manufacturing something is not a prerequisite to the production of wealth in a global economy. For example, if I sell a math book that has been sitting on my shelf to someone for twenty-five dollars, two things happen. I now have twenty-five bucks in my pocket and the buyer has the math book. Everyone wins. Wealth is enhanced; yet, nothing was produced except a trade.

SPECIAL INTEREST GROUPS

Bashing and baiting law abiding citizens has galvanized special interest groups. Allowing gays in the military, attacking the Catholic church and Protestant evangelicals, muzzling pro-life speech, pushing condoms for school kids, and banning "bad" rifles are a few of the issues that have united special interest groups.

These single-issue groups have one thing in common. Big, coercive government has them running scared and hopping mad. Forcing one group to pay for something they find morally objectionable, for example, or depriving another group of rights they believe constitutionally guaranteed is nonsensical. People are awakening to the tyrannical potential of unlimited government and a tyranny by the majority.

These single-issue groups have one thing in common. Big, coercive government has them running scared and hopping mad.

A complementary factor is that some of these interest groups are viewed by the establishment, in particular the belt-way crowd in the nation's capitol, as politically incorrect. That is, they are frequently seen as being out of step with the East Coast/California politically correct liberalism that dominates the news media and entertainment industry.

There is the so-called Christian right, for example, which incurs the wrath of the media, Hollywood, and other anointed types. But those same people think it proper that people pay taxes to support the National Endowment for the Arts sponsorship of Robert Maplethorpe's "art" and his "PissChrist," a rendering of Christ encased in urine. Or, that they should be required, along with others opposed to abortion ("right to life" groups), to pay taxes to fund abortions they find morally wrong.

The liberal politicians are playing with dynamite when they rant and rave about the "radical" Christian right. Vice President Quayle won the "Murphy Brown" exchange. These folks happen to be mostly hard working, honest citizens with traditional family values, who pay their taxes and do more than their share of good works.

Another group happens to believe that the Second Amendment to the Constitution means exactly what it says: "The right of the people to keep and bear arms, shall not be infringed." The so-called "gun lobby," a large, single issue interest group, like many Christians, also fears the centralized power of the federal government. If semi-automatic rifles, then why not pistols? If the Second Amendment goes, then why not the First or the Fourth or the Fifth? Gun owners, whatever their purposes, would seem to have some justification for their worries, given the almost universal belief that criminals will still get their guns with or without "gun control" legislation.

A cartoon in the *Wall Street Journal* on August 23rd, 1994 showed two politicians walking in front of the Nation's Capitol saying, "Of course I favor a national anti-gun law. Who wants armed taxpayers?"

The existence of these and other single-issue organizations, such as those involved in the term limit movement and the flat tax movement, have a growing awareness of similarities in their circumstances. The tyrannical use of government might produce unexpected coalitions of voters. Reeling from the liberal establishment's disregard of their deeply held moral convictions, anti-abortionists might find themselves more sympathetic to the attack on gun owners. Those on the Christian "right" who are made sport of because they are committed to family values and opposed to welfare programs which undermine these values might sympathize with members of the National Rifle Association (NRA).

The uniting of these various coalitions might spark a revolution. Thomas Jefferson once said, "Whenever the people are well informed, they can be trusted with their government; whenever things get so far wrong as to attract their notice (the people) may be relied on to set them right." The role of the Constitution was clearly enunciated by our founders: to protect freedom from democracy and the individual from the majority.

BUSINESS BASHING

Bashing business is bad business, bad politics, and about to blow the lid off the tea kettle.

Estimates are that regulatory burdens on industry and individuals exceed $600 billion a year, about 10 percent of the Gross Domestic Product. The costs of environmental regulations alone exceed $100 billion. We can expect that American industry and therefore the American people are simply not going to take it any more.

As the National Federation of Independent Businesses (NFIB) regularly reminds the President and Congress, these costs are especially burdensome for small and medium sized businesses. Look, for example, at the impact of "threshold" rules that mandate employers take some sort of action when the number of their workers goes beyond a certain level. At least twelve federal laws impose threshold compliance costs on small businesses, including, for example, the Civil Rights Act of 1964, the Age Discrimination Employment Act of 1967, the Employee Retirement Income Security Act (ERISA) of 1974, the Occupational Safety and Health Act of 1970, the Americans With Disabilities Act of 1990, and the Clean Air Act Amendments of 1990.

As consultant Clark Judge reported, "The list of federal laws with thresholds reads like a Who's Who of regulatory horror shows." The burdens are particularly oppressive because of the incomprehensible bureaucratic maze that a business faces when attempting to comply with the law, no matter how bad.

A reason for optimism revolves around the backlash from liberals' practice of demonizing American business. Hillary Rodham Clinton has demonstrated an affinity for business bashing. She has accused the pharmaceutical industry of profiteering and price gouging and has also offered similar views of physicians and insurance companies. Of course, the Clinton Administration accuses anyone who became wealthy in the 1980s—people like Bill Gates of Microsoft and Sam Walton of Wal-Mart—of being greedy Reagan Republicans. Given Mrs. Clinton's $100,000 "profit" in the commodities market, it all sounds a bit self-serving, not to say embarrassing, for the administration.

The American people are not as dumb as liberals seem to believe. Bashing American business, where most of us

still work and earn our livelihood, is at minimum bad
politics. At worst (best) it could provide the igniting spark
to re-ignite the original American dream of liberty and
limited government.

TOO MANY FEDERAL IMPOSITIONS

Bashing State and Local government could backfire on
the feds.

The federal government has fallen in love with the
practice of mandating tasks to be accomplished by state
and local governments and/or the private sector. However,
the costs of compliance and enforcement of these federal
decisions are not borne by the federal government. Given
the taxpayers opposition to higher tax rates and the federal
budgetary control agreements in recent years, beginning
with Gramm-Rudman in the 1980s, Congress has been
sorely tempted to expand its power on the cheap—not
through federal appropriations of more money and,
therefore, higher taxes, but through mandates on others.

During the 1980s, Congress passed more than twenty-
five major laws with new, unfunded regulatory burdens
for state and local governments. As the *Wall Street
Journal* reported, "Anger has been building among voters
about the high handed way in which the Imperial Congress
decrees that state and local governments must perform
certain tasks—without providing the money to perform
them."

The U.S. Conference of Mayors, National Association
of Counties, National League of Cities, and the
International City Management Association declared
October 27, 1993 "National Unfunded Mandates Day" to

protest. One estimate indicates that the local government costs of complying with environmental mandates of the Environmental Protection Agency (EPA) will be $32 billion by the year 2000. Another study by the National Association of Towns and Townships estimates the costs to cities of all unfunded federal mandates will be about $54 billion for the five year period 1994-98.

Governor Pete Wilson of California is suing the federal government for over $370 million in federally mandated costs of providing medical and other welfare benefits to illegal immigrants. Costs imposed on private business by federal mandates are also high but difficult to isolate from other regulatory burdens. We are talking about tens-of-billions of dollars.

The conclusion: It is no longer possible for big-government politicians to hide the tremendous costs of their desire to do good with other people's money.

Who would have guessed that state and local government would join the revolution on the side of the revolutionaries. It is a real possibility. Even government workers know how to toss tea, don't they?

STAND THERE OR SIC 'EM

David Frum has written one of the best books of the decade entitled *Dead Right*. In it he says, "Conservatives have lost their zeal for advocating minimal government not because they have decided big government is desirable, but because they have wearily concluded that trying to reduce it is hopeless, and that even the task of preventing its further growth will probably exceed their strength."

If that is true, friend, don't just do something! Stand there!

Fortunately, there is an alternative. Let me explain it with a story.

There is a woman who calls a repairman to fix her microwave oven. Expecting many dinner guests that evening and needing the oven, she tells the repairman she will be out for the afternoon and that the key to the front door is under the welcome mat.

The repairman arrives at the home, finds the key and enters the living room. Greeting him is an angry, growling Doberman and a large, caged parrot hollering "Polly says hello. Polly says hello."

Cautiously, the repairman backs his way into the kitchen to fix the microwave. The Doberman follows him step for step, growling incessantly. "Growl, growl." The parrot keeps screeching "Polly says hello. Polly says hello."

Finishing his work, the repairman carefully picks up his tools and makes his way to the front door. The growling dog and screaming parrot have, by now, pushed him to the end of his rope. As he steps out the front door, he looks up at the bird and shouts "You stupid bird! Can't you say something else?"

Feathers raised, the parrot screamed back "Sic 'em!"

Stand there? Or Sic 'em? Each of us is free to choose.

Thirty years ago, I voted in my first election. As a die-hard liberal, I was jubilant that Lyndon Johnson gave conservative Republican presidential opponent Barry Goldwater a land-slide trouncing.

Times have changed. So have I.

As good fortune would have it, my wife and I now live a few miles down Tatum Boulevard from Senator Goldwater. Long ago, he made a decision to sic 'em. I'll close this section with his challenge. For me, it is a clarion call. How about you?

> I have little interest in streamlining government or in making it more efficient, for I mean to reduce its size. I do not undertake to promote welfare, for I propose to extend freedom. My aim is not to pass laws, but to repeal them. It is not to inaugurate new programs, but to cancel old ones that do violence to the Constitution, or that have failed in their purpose, or that impose on the people an unwarranted financial burden. I will not attempt to discover whether legislation is "needed" before I have first determined whether it is constitutionally permissible. And if I should later be attacked for neglecting my constituents' "interests," I shall reply that I was informed that their main interest is liberty and in that cause I am doing the very best I can.[1]

PART III

WHAT IN THE WHITE HOUSE IS GOING ON?

Chapter Nine

THE CLINTON AGENDA

When Bill Clinton accepted the Democratic Party's nomination for the presidency in the summer of 1992, he made clear his intentions to use his position of power to run the economy. "I know how President Lincoln felt when General McClellan wouldn't attack in the Civil War. He asked him, 'If you're not going to use your army, may I borrow it?' And so I say, George Bush, if you won't use your power to help America, step aside. I will." [1]

Unfortunately, Clinton's agenda is flawed. Governmentalism is a failed promise. The centralists have lost touch. They are exhausted because their ideas are bankrupt. Helping people to become helpless is not an act of kindness no matter how much you care. Government cannot create jobs. Government does not protect the consumer. Government does not know how to run a business. Government does not know how to run a health club, let alone health care. Top down social engineering by government is a hopelessly inefficient throwback to the by-gone era of the Machine Age. It's over.

From the dawn of civilization the tension between politics and economics has been the tension between income growth and income distribution. Every society faces the same basic questions: Who should hold decision making power—buyers and sellers or government officials? When should government rules replace market prices? Where should economics end and politics begin? Or, in other words, who gets to choose? The Clinton people think it should be them. Empowered individuals think otherwise.

THE GRAND DESIGNERS

President Clinton is a politician. He has always worked for government. He believes in government. As such, he has had to concoct a myriad of political remedies that he sees as solutions to your problems. The essence of practical politics, after all, is to dredge up a crisis and then call for a government solution.

If the Clinton Administration were a stage play, it would drive the audience mad. The incongruity between the words spoken on the stage and the words spoken off would be too great to bear.

On stage, the President says he feels your pain, understands your problems and resonates with audiences large and small. Off stage, the reality is much different.

Clinton lacks foundational beliefs, has a penchant for government "by bull session," is responsible for the continuing chaos in the White House, has a foreign policy that is terminally ad hoc—almost always responding to events, is constantly ensnared by his careless campaign rhetoric, and is ill-advised by the far left element of the Democratic Party. Adding fuel to the fire, he is an insecure man with a volcanic temper.

But Clinton's temper is the least of our problems. The problem is policy and the ideas of the people that produce them. The Clinton Administration is full of liberal activists wanting to do good with other people's money.

Hillary Rodham Clinton has Rooseveltian ambitions. "I'm not interested in attending a lot of funerals around the world. I want maneuverability. . . . I want to get deeply involved in solving problems," she says.[2] Her influence is widespread throughout the Administration. She's accountable to no one.

The first lady criticizes greed, but involves herself in the cattle futures market to turn $1,000 into $100,000. She says she's for small business. But, when asked about the cost of her health care plan's cost on small business, she replies, "I can't go out and save every under capitalized entrepreneur in America." In a speech at the University of Texas entitled "A Crisis of Meaning," Mrs. Clinton suggested that our country was suffering a "sleeping sickness of the soul." She talked of alienation and despair, and hopelessness and loss of values. But during the 1992 Presidential campaign, when Republicans were trying to stress family values, she said, "American women don't need lectures from Washington about values."

An aide who works with her daily was asked about the contradiction of criticizing those talking about values. "Hillary's a lawyer, not a philosopher," the aide said. "She contradicts herself because she's very good at giving arguments on both sides. She could give the lecture on why lectures on values shouldn't be given and turn around and give the lecture on values—both with equal effectiveness."

Hmmmm.

"I suppose I could have stayed home and baked cookies and had teas," she said during the presidential campaign. But the real indication of her world view came in her interview with *Glamour* magazine in April of 1993. "It's so hard," she said, "to keep people's attention focused on what will matter in their own lives."

Mommy, what's the definition of paternalism?

Vice President Al Gore is also full of government solutions. Although the press has scrambled to portray him as an environmental "moderate," a close look shows he is quite radical. The outline of his radical environmental vision is found in his book *Earth In the Balance: Ecology and the Human Spirit,* suggesting throughout that the earth is on the verge of environmental apocalypse.

As with everybody in this administration, looming catastrophe demands radical government solutions. Mr. Gore wants a "strategic environment initiative" that would use the tax code and regulation to phase out the "old technologies." And although he flatly denied it in his 1992 debate with then Vice President Dan Quayle, he wants a "Global Marshall Plan" of at least $100 billion to pay for much of this. And, he would require the wealthy nations like the U.S. to allocate money for transferring environmentally helpful technologies to the Third World.

The 1994 International Conference on Population and Development held in Cairo, Egypt for the first time had the backing and support of the U.S. government. In a break with past presidents, President Clinton and Vice President Gore pledged U.S. tax money to support international population control efforts, including birth control, sterilization and abortion.

Robert Reich, Clinton's Secretary of Labor and Ira Magaziner, the designer of the Clinton's health care monstrosity, have earlier co-authored a book entitled *Minding America's Business: The Decline and Rise of the American Economy*. Because the world economy is prone to sudden changes, they write, "Active government policies are necessary to enable the economy to respond quickly and efficiently to worldwide structural changes. Government officials must have a vision of the overall structural development of the international economy and a thorough knowledge of the products, markets and competitive dynamics of individual businesses." [3]

Can anyone who is even the least familiar with the workings of business not laugh at such a statement? Where is the evidence that representative governments can respond quickly and efficiently to anything? Magaziner and Reich say that all government must know is international structure, products, markets, and competitive dynamics of individual business. Is that all these mortal bureaucrats need to know? It takes your breath away; an all knowing, fact finding, omniscient, omnipotent, tripartite committee composed of gods. The impossibility and arrogance of such a sentence defies description. Yet, Reich and Magaziner are the very soul of this administration.

For the first time in the history of the United States, the Secretary of Agriculture had no background in production agriculture. Although Mike Espy has now been relieved of his job for accepting gifts and perks barred by ethics laws, it is significant that President Clinton did not feel it necessary for the person who represents farmers to ever have been a farmer.

Clinton says he wants his cabinet to look like America. Does a black attorney, a Spanish attorney, a female attorney, and a half dozen white attorneys, all educated at the elite schools, look like America to you? He says he wants more women in the White House. Yet his Senior Staff of Gore, Rubin, Panetta, McLarty, etc. are all male. Republican strategist Bill Kristol puts this issue in sharp focus: "The problem is not the white boys in the inner circle, the problem is the white boy in the middle of the circle."

The polish on those chosen to accomplish the Clinton agenda is wearing thin. White House counsel Barnard Nussbaum and Treasury officials Roger Altman and Jean Hanson were history after questions were raised about their conduct in the Whitewater inquiries. White House administrator David Watkins was fired after taking a presidential helicopter to play golf. Associate Attorney General Webster Hubbell quit shortly after he was discovered to have over-billed his Arkansas law firm. In December of 1994, Hubbell pleaded guilty to mail fraud and income tax evasion. Kenneth Starr, the Whitewater special prosecutor, said Hubbell swindled the Rose Hill Law Firm and some of its clients of at least $394,000. Henry Cisneros, Housing and Urban Development Secretary is being probed to determine if he was truthful on payments to his ex-mistress.

There are others. Ron Brown, Donna Shalala, Stanley Greenberg, Joycelyn Elders (now fired, and there will be more), James Carville, George Stephanopoulos, Janet Reno, Mandy Grunwald, Laura D'Andrea Tyson, and dozens more who, if you had to describe them in a word, it would be liberal. In two words, very liberal.

CHALLENGING THE AGENDA

The Clinton agenda, challenged in this section, exerts enormous power over our daily lives. It is not a plan to change America at the margin. The power these designers want for government is overwhelming and all encompassing.

I want to identify the most threatening of their plans, explain the alternatives, and watch the ever alert American public insist on market, rather than government, solutions.

We will examine the Administration's ideas by quoting their words. And then, as an antidote, use epigrams, parody, humor and common sense to reveal what most of you already know: The emperor has no clothes.

Chapter Ten

HEALTH CARE

"Health care should be a right, not a privilege." [1]

-Bill Clinton

James Madison, a founding father and major contributor to the final draft of the Constitution of the United States, was adamantly opposed to universal rights. Indeed, he probably would have walked out of the convention had the authors written positive rights like food, health care and education into the Constitution. He understood that once you pretend the notion of universal rights, freedom is everywhere jeopardized.

Madison insisted on the unalienable rights to life, liberty and the pursuit of happiness. The underlying idea for the Constitution, the Bill of Rights, and the formation of three branches of government was to protect freedom from democracy and the individual from the majority.

All legitimate rights have one thing in common. They impose no obligation on other people—only the negative obligation to leave you alone. Our political system was originally designed to give everybody a chance to work for what they wanted. It was not a guarantee to receive something from somebody else without effort.

Thomas Jefferson said, "To take from one, because it is thought his own industry and that of his fathers has acquired too much, in order to spare to others who, or whose fathers have not exercised equal industry and skill, is to violate arbitrarily the first principles of association, the guarantee to everyone the free exercise of his industry and the fruits acquired by it."

In the continuing debate over health care we have neglected to discuss the insights of Madison, Jefferson and other founding fathers.

The United States of America was founded on the proposition that individuals possess rights that are "unalienable." They are not favors granted by government. They are rights of action derived from individual membership in the human community or, as our founding fathers said, God-given. Individuals cannot be used against their will to satisfy the goals of others.

Unfortunately, we have seen an almost complete abandonment of these moral principles, and a wholly opposite view of rights has come to prevail. Today, individuals are *entitled* to make demands on others. Rights are thus legislated which enslave those who are required to contribute to the goals of others.

What really happens when government takes from Sue and gives to Dwight?

If Sue's dues are Dwight's rights, is liberty for belles really what it's cracked up to be?

When a law bestows a right,
it rightfully should be,
enjoyed by every single soul,
that's equality.

But when the law grants privilege,
it's time for you to fret,
if you're the one who's got to give,
while others git to get.

Take health care by the government.
When these accrue to Dwight,
and bills for same are sent to Sue,
that's not an equal right.

Such laws should be repealed at once,
legislatively.
In search of equal rights for Sue,
let's E-R-A-s-e.

- OBSERVATION -

So long as Sue's dues remain Dwight's rights,
Sue will remain an indentured servant.

WE CAN HAVE GOVERNMENT HEALTH CARE WITHOUT LOSS OF FREEDOM???

"I'm such a government junkie." [2]

-Hillary Rodham Clinton

The First Lady claims her plan is based on security, simplicity, savings, choice, quality, and health care that's always there. In fact, it is a scheme about asserting government power and limiting personal choice. In page after mind-numbing page the plan threatens consumers, limits the way health care suppliers can compete and practice medicine, slows medical innovation, rejects the use of market incentives and raises taxes to boot.

If you think that insurance companies create paperwork, just wait till you read the now defunct Rube Goldberg monstrosity cooked up by Ira Magaziner and the First Lady.

American politicians cannot resist the paternalistic control of peoples' lives. Unfortunately, it is individual freedom that is sacrificed on the altar of collectivism. Through mandates, managed competition, gatekeepers, regional health alliances, price controls and enforcement mechanisms like require, limit, penalize, prohibit, restrict, sanction, prison, fine and ban, the unalienable liberties espoused by our founding fathers are crushed by the stampede of governmentalists attempting to take care of us.

Forsooth, forsooth,
I lost a tooth
in a stick of gum one day.
Forsooth, forsooth,
without my tooth
what would the Clintons say?

Oh! From their great big white house,
this problem is no puzzle.
Their answer here was crystal clear,
"gum chewers need a muzzle!"

Then folks replied
from Wrigley's side.
"Gum chewing," they asserted,
"is such an old established right
it mustn't be deserted."

But in the halls of Congress
special interests held no sway.
Health care laws were drafted
and mouth belts saved the day.

And so, throughout this land of ours,
where health care laws are made,
all teeth are cleaned by government.
Only freedom has decayed.

The Clinton paternalism is a lethal one; a question of life or death. If the central planners in Moscow could not get food to the grocery stores, how can we expect that well-meaning government health planners would correctly decide how many radiologists and gynecologists we should have? How many of you would be in favor of returning to 1960 health spending levels and, therefore, do without bypass operations, CAT scans, MRI's, PETT scans, endoscopes, and laser microsurgery? Wouldn't gatekeepers have an incentive to limit access to specialists and high-tech medicine? Do you really want the greatest health care system in the world to come under the control of political bureaucracies?

A federal judge requested documents pertaining to Hillary's health care task force's work in order to rule on the legality of the secrecy being maintained by the group. The task force responded that deliberations were disorganized and that complete records had not been kept. In other words, the Clintons want to micro-manage America's health care, a major part of the economy, even though they were unable to organize the task force charged with planning it. Humorist P. J. O'Rourke captures the essence of what we were denied: "We are not allowed to watch Hillary's Gang of 500 presumably for the same reason we should not watch the manufacture of sausage."

Now a battle rages over whether the United States will put government in charge of everyone's health care. The Clintons' health care plan would make it a crime to obtain alternative, private coverage. Similar to communism's single choice, one party, one point of view, one make of car, so does this plan limit us all to just a few choices.

Magaziner vehemently denied just one benefits package. He argued every American will have three to choose from. Seriously, he was proud there were three. Ira, try three thousand or three million. That's how many the market would offer and that is how many people would want.

The Canadian situation hints at what will happen. In Canada, universal coverage is modified by "delisting" (no longer covering) certain procedures as costs explode, and the rationing process becomes more severe. Under the Clinton and Mitchell health care plan, consumers would find their ability to choose their doctors and coverage severely limited, if not completely denied.

The health care reform debate is really about two competing visions of the society in which we wish to live. Do we prefer voluntary, market solutions with limited government to guarantee a free society of sovereign and responsible individuals? Or, do we prefer a collectivist kindergarten in which we are treated as wards of the state? While Hillary Rodham Clinton, at every stage of the health care debate, clung to bureaucratic health care solutions, most Americans expressed their desire to reverse this drift to the left. Isn't it about time we restore the original American dream in human liberty?

- OBSERVATION -

Ask not from government and you may save your ask!
Ask from government and you will surely lose it!

THE EVIL PHARMACEUTICAL INDUSTRY

On May 26, 1993, Hillary was speaking to a group of hospital and nursing home employees. She criticized the *"price gouging, cost shifting, and unconscionable profiteering"* of the pharmaceutical industry. [3]

-Hillary Rodham Clinton

The medication Scott must take
was banned from use today.
It causes diarrhea
in mice—or so they say.

So Scott must trot to Denmark
to buy his medication.
If left up to the Clinton folks,
he'll die of constipation.

But wait! Pharmaceutical therapy is our most efficient form of health care.

Drug therapy for coronary artery disease costs about $1,000 a year compared to $41,000 for bypass surgery. Drug therapy for ulcers costs $900 a year compared to $25,000 for surgery. Drug therapy for depression costs $5,000 a year compared to $73,000 for institutionalization.

Since 1965, drug costs have increased more slowly than any other type of medical care. The average out-of-pocket cost per person for drugs is $232 a year, less than in most other industrialized countries. But, because health insurance usually covers 80 to 100 percent of hospital and physician costs and only 60 percent of drug costs, a patient may pay more out-of-pocket for $1,000 worth of heart medicine than for a $41,000 by-pass.

Sensitivity to out-of-pocket drug costs has led to proposals for pharmaceutical price controls. If all drug profits were eliminated, health care spending would decrease less than 2 percent. However, the $10 billion a year that drug companies invest in developing new drugs and other products would fall dramatically.

Science has led to a greater understanding of the causes of disease and potential cures. At the same time, the pharmaceutical marketplace has become more competitive, creating pressure on both prices and earnings. Breakthrough drugs soon find competitors and generic alternatives commanding a growing share of the market.

To survive, pharmaceutical companies have had to restructure and devote billions of dollars to innovative drug and biotechnology research. The Office of Technology Assessment estimates that it costs $359 million to develop a single new drug and fewer than 1 in 10 companies recover this cost.

By eliminating profit incentives we may save money in the short run, but at the cost of denying millions of people quicker access to drugs that can save their lives.

The problem, of course, is the way we pay for health care. It encourages patients and doctors to choose the most expensive therapies when cheaper alternatives would have been just as effective, or more so.

On the average, patients pay out-of-pocket only 4.5 cents of every dollar they spend on hospital care and only 16.5 cents of every dollar they spend on physician services. By contrast, they pay 68.3 cents out-of-pocket for every dollar they spend on pharmaceuticals.

To patients, therefore, hospital therapy often appears cheaper than drug therapy, although for society as a whole the opposite may be true. A patient may choose a $29,000 operation for ulcers over a $900 drug treatment because the operation only costs the patient $250 out-of-pocket whereas the entire $900 for drugs may be an out-of-pocket cost.

Under ClintonCare, a presidential appointee would control the price of every new drug, based on its development cost and profitability. But for every profitable drug developed there are a thousand which don't make it. Who is going to decide? The problem with ClintonCare is not just that government thinks it knows best, but the preposterous notion that government thinks it can know everything relevant.

Of course, as we already mentioned at the opening of Part III, Ira Magaziner, the grand designer of the Grand Designers, thinks that "active government must have a vision of the overall structural development of the international economy and a thorough knowledge of the products, markets, and competitive dynamics of individual business."

Compared to that, running one-seventh of the U.S. economy should be no problem.

CONTROL COSTS BY MANAGING CARE?

"People who are not now insured, and the companies they work for, are going to pay a lot more [for health security]. That's a matter of equity." [4]

-Ira Magaziner

Ira is a forceful speaker
and he toughened up his drawl.

He's announced a second coming
in time to save "you all."

He asked for our suggestions
to halt health care's ills.

Respectfully, may we propose
fewer Ira planning pills!

"If you're looking for a social engineer, Ira is the best there is," says my friend Michael Rothschild. But the era of social engineering ended with the Machine Age.

Magaziner's answer to the problem of cost escalation in the Medicare and Medicaid programs is to make the whole health care system into one big Medicaid program. Managed care and the use of gatekeepers to ration health care, we are told, are the answers to runaway costs. And this, in spite of the bureaucratic failure of price controls and other non-price rationing of health care services in the existing Medicare and Medicaid programs.

The real problem is ignored, undoubtedly because it is not understood. If the money price of a good or service that people value is made zero, then consumption will soar. Called the law of demand, this proposition explains much of human behavior. When prices go down, the amount demanded goes up. And when prices are reduced to zero, the amount demanded really goes up. Given existing supplies, common sense tells us that costs too will rise.

The crisis in the American health care system is that health care services are often viewed by the patient-consumer as being free or close to it. Ninety-five percent of hospital bills are paid by third parties, a government agency, an insurance company or an employer. Over 80 percent of physician service fees are paid by third parties. With low-deductible, low co-payment bells-and-whistles policies being subsidized by the federal tax code, the health care consumption decisions of individuals are divorced from the costs that they ultimately must bear.

Prepaid managed care programs, mainly Health Maintenance Organizations (HMO's), strive to control costs. They do so not by forcing patients to recognize the costs they impose on the entire health care system, but rather by rationing care to remain within predetermined budgets. Gatekeepers, frequently non-medically trained personnel, make these all-important decisions.

Unfortunately, the managed care health facility invariably charges a minimum out-of-pocket fee to the patient. Therefore, the fundamental and unavoidable problem remains: health care continues to be viewed as free or nearly free and the demand for medical services exceeds supply. Rationing of health care, then, becomes the only way to cope with the excess demand.

Until we empower consumers to spend their own money when making health care choices, individual responsibility will be lacking and the problems made worse by political solutions will not go away.

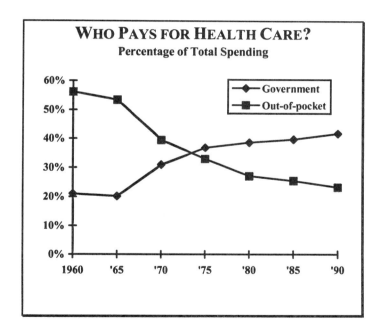

- OBSERVATION -

If you think health care is expensive now,
wait till you see what it costs when it's free!

THE SOLUTION TO AMERICA'S HEALTH CARE? "FREE" COVERAGE FOR ALL

-CLINTON CHANGE-

"Before this Congress finishes its work next year, you will pass, and I will sign, legislation to guarantee [health] security to every citizen of this country."

-Clinton, *WSJ*, 9/22/93

"If you send me legislation that does not guarantee every American private health insurance that can never be taken away, you will force me to take this pen [and] veto the legislation."

-Clinton, *WSJ*, 1/29/94

"If Congress passes a bill that is different from the one I originally proposed, would I veto it? . . . If it is a credible attempt to [achieve full coverage], then I'm open to it."

-Clinton, *WSJ*, 7/29/94

"I certainly don't want to embrace an approach that . . . won't achieve our objectives. [Let's] see what people are feeling like after they get a night's sleep or two."

-Clinton, *WSJ*, 8/26/94

Mr. President, we now know where you stand. Would you please recognize where most health care economists stand?[5]

Prices matter. Though people are not as price sensitive in the market for health care as they are in the markets for most other goods and services, they still consume more health care when prices are lower and less when prices are higher. In general, a 10 percent drop in the out-of-pocket price of medical services causes about a 4 percent increase in demand. And, a 10 percent drop in the price of health insurance—after adjusting for tax subsidies for employer-provided coverage causes about a 7 percent increase in demand.

Health care spending has been rising because prices paid by patients have been falling. Evidence suggests that when we are spending our own money, we are conservative, prudent shoppers in the medical marketplace. When we are using someone else's money, we consume much more.

Seventy-five percent of individual health care expenditures do not come from our own pockets. Medicare, Medicaid, insurance companies, and employers shield us from the true cost of health care. Over the last 30 years, the share of income spent out-of-pocket on health care has declined while the amount spent from all other sources has more than tripled., rising from 4.2 percent of consumption in 1960 to 13.3 percent in 1990.

Most Americans are over-insured because of government policies. We over-rely on third-party payers because, through generous tax subsidies, government "pays" up to one-half of the cost of employer-provided health insurance and, through Medicaid and Medicare, government directly pays medical bills for the poor and the elderly.

The main cause of rising health care spending is government, which now spends more than half of our health care dollars. People who look to government to solve our health policy problems may be unaware of how large a role the government already plays.

Direct government spending has increased from 21 percent of all health care spending in 1960 to 42 percent in 1990. When tax subsidies are included, the government's share of health care spending has increased from 34 percent in 1960 to 53 percent today.

Because of third-party insurance and government subsidies, the cost of health care is largely hidden from American families. Most people have no idea how much they personally are contributing to cover the nation's health care costs. In 1992, national health care spending was equal to $8,821 for every U.S. household. This burden, however, was largely disguised.

For an average working-age family, the visible outlays were $1,715 for out-of-pocket expenses and $726 for health insurance premiums. These direct expenses amounted to only about one-fourth of total health care spending per family, with the remainder hidden in taxes and reduced wages.

Because of government policy, many Americans are uninsured. In 1990 government "spent" about $64 billion subsidizing private health insurance through the tax system. Ostensibly, the subsidies encourage private health insurance coverage, but they probably do more harm than good. Why? Because the largest tax subsidies go to those who need them least—people who probably would purchase health insurance without any tax encouragement.

In addition, current tax laws penalize people who purchase their own health insurance, because they must do it with after-tax dollars.

Another problem is that tax laws encourage an employer-based system under which people who switch jobs can lose their coverage and become uninsurable after they get sick.

Lastly, the current system shelters the largest employers from the cost-increasing effects of state regulations while leaving individuals and small businesses vulnerable. Make no mistake about it. Government programs, regulations, policies, subsidies, and unequal tax treatments that penalize certain people are the main cause of our health care problems.

MEDICAL SAVINGS ACCOUNTS

Most health care economists agree that the solution is Medical Savings Accounts.[6]

All across the country, private employees are discovering a new way of controlling health care costs. It works so well that at some companies health care costs are actually going down. The secret: giving employees incentives to economize and to be disciplined shoppers.

More than a decade ago, for example, the Rand Corporation discovered that when people are spending their own money on health care they spend 30 percent less with no adverse effects on their health. Some employers are putting this principle to work.

For instance, Quaker Oats had a high-deductible policy and paid $300 annually into the personal health accounts of employees, who got to keep any unspent balance. The result? Over the past decade, the company's health care costs grew at an average of 6.3 percent per year, while premiums for the rest of the nation grew at double digit rates.

Forbes Magazine pays each employee 42 cents for every $1 of medical claims they do not incur up to a maximum of $1,000. The result? *Forbes* health costs fell 17 percent in 1992 and 12 percent in 1993.

Dominion Resources, a utility holding company, deposits $1,620 a year into a bank account for the 80 percent of employees who choose a $3,000 deductible. The result? The company has experienced no premium increase since 1989, while other employers faced annual increases of 13 percent.

Golden Rule Insurance Company deposits $2,000 a year into a Medical Savings Account for each employee who chooses a $3,000 family deductible. The result? In 1993, the first year of the plan, health costs were 40 percent lower than they otherwise would have been.

Under most proposals, individuals and their employers could make regular, tax-free deposits to MSA's, which would be the property of the individuals. They could withdraw money, without penalty, only to pay medical expenses or health insurance premiums. Money they did not spend would grow with interest, and they could use it for medical expenses after retirement, roll it over into an IRA or pension plan, or leave it as part of their estate.

Medical Savings Accounts would give individuals a new way to pay for health care. Under traditional health insurance, people make monthly premium payments to an insurer such as Blue Cross and the insurer pays medical bills as they are incurred. Under the new system, people could confine health insurance to catastrophic coverage (say, expenses above $3,000), reduce their monthly insurance premium payments and make deposits to a Medical Savings Account instead. Insurance would pay for expensive treatments that occur infrequently, while individuals would use their MSA funds to pay small bills covering routine services. After all, you don't use your auto insurance to pay for an oil change.

Chapter Eleven

WEALTH AND POVERTY

"Today, as we stand on the threshold of a new era, a new millennium, I believe we need a new kind of leadership, leadership committed to change. Leadership not mired in the politics of the past, not limited by old ideologies. Proven leadership that knows how to reinvent government to help solve the real problems of real people." [1]

-Bill Clinton

In ancient Greece, Pericles inaugurated the feeding of the people by using money taken in taxes. One hundred years later Plato found that he (Pericles) had so completely debauched the Athenians that they were reduced to pauperism. Instead of working, they loafed. Their characters were so weakened that the state was forced to hire barbarians to defend itself from invasion.

A paternalistic government is bound to destroy the self-reliance and self-respect of people. The self-interested person will usually take the easiest route to get what they want. If the easiest method of acquisition is that of production, they will produce. If there is some easier way, they will pursue it. From the beginning of time there has always been two ways to make a living. One way is to work. The other way is to steal.

Don't laugh. Stealing is a great labor saving device.

When personal responsibility goes, everything goes. It is a virtue which has made our country great and it alone will keep us great. Abraham Lincoln said, "You cannot strengthen the weak by weakening the strong. You cannot build character and courage by taking away man's initiative and independence. You cannot help men permanently by doing for them what they could and should do for themselves."

What happens when government taxes Peter to help Paul?

First, Peter becomes a Paul-bearer.

Second, Paul becomes an immovable object. When you pay people not to work, they don't work.

And third, piggyback replaces baseball as the national pastime.

- OBSERVATION -

When Paul-bearers peter out,
both Peter and Paul will go without!

Today, Americans are required to work from January through May just to pay their taxes, while an astonishing number of citizens, one in two, receive regular payments from some entity of government. Transfer payments which tax Peter to aid Paul heighten the prospective certainty of economic break-down.

What happened to poor people before Roosevelt's New Deal, Johnson's Great Society, and Clinton's New Covenant? The answer is most were helped by private-sector charities. Cities used to have thousands of volunteer charity workers, most, but not all, from religious organizations.

The 19th-century system was far from perfect, but it served a social function. Private charity workers believed they were their brothers' keepers. Welfare was not an entitlement.

The welfare system has become a trap for many poor people who receive benefits. Above a certain level, welfare payments provide a strong incentive for relatively low-skilled persons to accept welfare rather than to work. Despite a quarter-century of rising welfare payments and income levels, more Americans live in poverty today than twenty years ago. According to the latest government numbers, 39.3 million people are living in poverty.

In California, for example, a mother and two children might get $7,800 per year in welfare payments and another $6,000 worth of benefits such as Medicaid and food stamps. Taking a job for $7 per hour ($14,000 for 50 weeks' work) would make her family "nonpoor," but would provide only $200 more income per year. And there would be expenses associated with working. She would very likely choose to remain on welfare.[2]

She's trapped. What started out as a war on poverty has in reality become a war on the poor. All government can give is money. While money offers indefinite welfare payments, it also removes the cost of not working. While money (Medicaid) removes the barrier to hypochondria, it also takes away the incentive to stay healthy. While money offers drug rehabilitation, it simultaneously reduces the cost of addiction. While money allows welfare mothers to have more babies, it also encourages promiscuity. While money (Head Start) tries to give some kids a jump on learning, it also removes the responsibility for early training.

In short, government money enables people to do things they should not do without immediately suffering the consequences. Is that really what people need? Or, is it love, time, care, and hope? Should people be responsible for their decisions? Do people need a safety net or would they prefer an opportunity elevator?

- OBSERVATION -

Helping people to become helpless
is not an act of kindness.

WE NEED MORE POLITICIANS LIKE CLINTON. HE'S ALWAYS WILLING TO LEND A HELPING HAND

"'The highlight of my campaign was the Richmond debate when I talked to the woman,' Clinton said, referring to the questioner from the audience who had asked Clinton, Bush and Perot how the deficit had affected each of them personally. Bush had acted as though the question was from Mars and totally muffed it. Clinton had walked toward the woman and replied smoothly that he knew people in Arkansas who were unemployed and whose businesses were suffering, conveying empathy and understanding. 'Americans respond to specificity and a human touch.'" [3]

-Bill Clinton

During that same debate in Richmond, a young man with a pony-tail asked this question of the candidates. He said, "We are your children, we have our needs. What will you do to take care of us—to take care of our needs?" Each candidate—Bush, Clinton, Perot—fell over themselves telling what government could do.

Later, William Bennett, former Drug Czar and Secretary of Education offered these poignant comments about this episode: "Wouldn't it have been great if one of the candidates had said, 'Just a minute. Get a life. I am not your father. This is America, a do-it-yourself society. See a minister, see a priest, see your wife. Take care of yourself, man; get a hold of yourself."

But when people seek help, President Clinton is invariably responsive. He feels their pain. The result: health care for everybody, food stamp programs for needy students, grants for aspiring artists, loans for promising business ventures, subsidized housing for impoverished homeseekers, public work and training projects for the unemployed. You name it, and Clinton will have a government program for it.

On election day, throngs of grateful voters trudge to the polls. Few forget Clinton's helping hand.

Generally overlooked, however, in assessing the President's record of generosity is the Inexorable Rule of Thumb which holds: Ask politicians to lend a helping hand and you will never get a firm grasp on government spending. America is suffering from a multi-trillion dollar case of the grip!

═══════════════

Shake hands with the President . . .

His palms are soft.
His grip lacks clout.
Yet he wins votes
with each hand out.

═══════════════

The candidate who uses his own money to buy votes, someone has said, is called corrupt. The one who promises to use someone else's money is called a liberal. And "liberalism" has been a powerful force in American politics.

-C. Lowell Harriss

There are some politicians who, if their constituents were cannibals, would promise them missionaries for dinner.

-H. L. Mencken

That friendliness and charity of our countrymen can always be relied upon to relieve their fellow citizens in misfortune. . . . Federal aid in such cases encourages the expectation of paternal care on the part of the government and weakens the sturdiness of our national character, while it prevents the indulgence among our people of that kindly sentiment and conduct which strengthens the bonds of a common brotherhood.

-Grover Cleveland

TAX THE RICH

Hillary was angry at what she called *"the unacceptable acquiescence in greed that had occurred during the 1980s."* [4]

-Hillary Rodham Clinton

In an April 18th, 1994 *Business Week* article, Hillary Clinton's success in business was noted. The reporters said that Hillary's aggressive investment strategy belies the image of a log cabin Democrat decrying "quick buck artists." She, in fact, was doing the same thing as all those yuppies who she said represented the decade of greed. How many people do you know who could put $2,014 in a telecom investment partnership and in a few short years have a return of $45,998? Have you ever parlayed $1,000 into nearly $100,000 in the cattle market? Hillary bashes pharmaceuticals, but that doesn't stop her from putting $90,000 in a hedge fund filled with health care stocks. The authors conclude: "But whatever the First Lady thinks of the go-go Reagan years, it's clear she wasn't above taking advantage of the opportunities they presented."

"The Shaq" of the Orlando Magic, Emmett Smith of the Dallas Cowboys, Sam Walton of Wal-Mart fame, and young Bill Gates of Microsoft all seem, according to many, to have a disproportionate amount of "stuff," to use comedian George Carlin's word. At the other end of the spectrum, are the homeless and the poor. The rest of us are in-between. Many, in the name of "social justice," demand that government heavily tax the rich and redistribute the spoils to the middle class and the poor.

Yet, most Americans have long believed that if someone acquires wealth and fortune, honestly and by hard work, and even when luck is a significant factor, they should be entitled to keep it. How, then, do we reconcile the envious mentality of taxing the rich and, generally most productive members of society?

Whether we like it or not, equality between individuals is not a characteristic of the human community and is, therefore, unattainable. We differ by genetic factors and environmental influences. We differ with respect to our abilities and work ethic to achieve material well-being. And we also differ with regard to life styles, personalities, physical dexterity, life expectancy, and among many, many other characteristics.

Even if we taxed away all or most of The Shaq's income each year, unequal incomes would continue to arise. Professional basketball players make more money than most of us. The reason? Millions of people voluntarily pay lots of money to watch them play. To maintain an equality of incomes, therefore, would require a continuous and never-ending rearrangement of income shares. But high tax rates and the on-going intervention in the economy to achieve equality discourages work effort, saving and investment. Nevertheless, moved by the acids of envy and what Hillary calls "greed," governments relentlessly tax the efforts of the most productive.

Shaquille O'Neal, you're too unnerving.
Your high-rise jumps are too self-serving.

No one should leap when lesser lads
can't get off their launching pads.

No one should hang, high in the air
flaunting skills amid despair.

No one should dunk when gimpy moles
must go without high flying soles.

Ground level is for everyone.
Should privileged folk have all the fun?

Since earthbound scrubs have little thrust
Someone should act from anti-trust.

Rules must be made to check all hovers
to equalize downtrodden brothers.

No one should soar when lowly dregs
are held to earth by short man's legs!

Equality of outcome is impossible precisely because
we are not equal.

The problem rests with our conflicting views of what
justice in the distribution of material well-being means.
What is a fair division of all that stuff?

Much of the nineteenth and twentieth centuries debate has been dominated by those who want end-state principles of distributive justice. Equality is defined and measured with regard to how the game ends. Those who favor end-state principles believe it is fair to redistribute income shares after the actual outcome of a competitive market process.

The other major view of distributive justice favors process principles. Equality and fairness are measured in terms of how the game is played. For example, in a private property, market economy, government's role is to enforce the rules of exchange. Contracts are enforced. Fraud and violence are prevented. In other words, anything that is peaceful is OK. If the rules of the game have been established by a social compact like common law or the U.S. Constitution, and if an individual, say Bill Gates of Microsoft, plays by the rules, then he is entitled to his $10 billion. Of course, the game is never over, and we don't know whether it will end with Mr. Gates in or out of *Forbes* list of the richest individuals in America.

We have lost our bearings concerning equality of outcome. Following President Clinton's 1993 tax hike, many Americans have tax rates of around 60 percent (39.6 percent Federal income tax, 15.3 percent FICA/Medicare, and a state income tax). The overwhelming majority of these people played by the rules of the game. Then, at the end of the game (April 15th), 60 percent of their income is confiscated in the name of equality and social justice.

- OBSERVATION -

"Government taxes work, production, savings and investment. They subsidize leisure and consumption. Should we be surprised that we get less of the first and more of the second?"

-David R. Henderson.

WE MUST REVERSE THE REAGAN/BUSH YEARS AND THE DECADE OF GREED

"We hope to create more millionaires than Ronald Reagan ever did—but they'll have to pay their fair share in taxes."[5]

-Bill Clinton

Soon after the Clinton budget was passed, Clinton and twenty members of his administration staged a symbolic reenactment of the event. James Carville, one of Clinton's wealthiest friends, was bent over Clinton's Oval Office desk, and his wallet was removed. Clinton then proceeded to throw $20 bills around the room in an effort to "redistribute his wealth." [6]

Divide the wealth
and hand it out,
taxation is no sin.
When mine runs out
I plan to shout,
'Lets divvy up agin!
And agin! And agin!"

When federal aid is always authorized . . .
While income tax forms are scrutinized . . .
When profits breed suspicion . . .
While losses are subsidized . . .
When failure is rewarded . . .
While success is penalized . . .
When taxes take most all folks make . . .
The outcome is certain.

Eventually, everyone will go without!

- O B S E R V A T I O N -

The day may come when folks will say,
"We cannot share. Oh woe! Dismay!
For nothing much was made today."

The reason? Government has interfered with production by offering incentives to fail rather than to succeed; to consume rather than to produce; to stagnate rather than to achieve.

During the 1992 Clinton campaign for President, Americans were repeatedly bombarded with reports of studies showing that the U.S. tax system had become increasingly unfair. These reports were mostly misleading and wrong. Among the myths propagated: [7]

Myth: During the 1980s, the rich got richer and the poor got poorer.

Fact: Every income class had a substantial increase in real after-tax income. The average increase in real income was 21.2 percent for every man, woman and child in the country.

Myth: The Reagan tax cuts were a giveaway to the rich.

Fact: Wealthy taxpayers increased their total tax payments and their share of tax payments.

The top 10 percent of earners paid more taxes after the tax rate cuts of 1981 and 1986, both as a percentage of the nation's total income taxes paid and in actual dollars.

In 1988, the top 10 percent paid about 57 percent of all income taxes, compared to 49.3 percent in 1980.

Why did high-income people pay more taxes after their rates were cut? The lower tax rates lured money out of tax shelters and reduced the attractiveness of tax deductible, business-related expenses. As a result, the net real income from partnerships and Subchapter S corporations, two types of businesses used for sheltering income from taxes, rose 360 percent, from $12 billion in 1980 to $56 billion in 1988. In addition, lower tax rates encouraged secondary workers (often spouses) in high-income families to work and earn more.

Myth: Reagan tax reform was unfair to low-income families.

Fact: As a result of the 1981 and 1986 Tax Acts, increases in personal exemptions and standard deductions made the income of 4 million low-income taxpayers non-taxable. Those still paying taxes have lower taxes than they would have had without tax reform. For example, low and moderate-income families would pay 40 percent more in income and payroll taxes if the 1980 tax law were still in effect today.

Myth: The income tax system has become less progressive during the 1980s.

Fact: The share of taxes paid by the top 5 percent of taxpayers rose from 37.6 percent to 45.9 percent. The top 10 percent of income earners now pay about 57 percent of all income taxes—up from 49.5 percent. The share paid by the bottom half of income earners fell from 6.8 percent to 5.5 percent.

Chapter Twelve

JOBS AND ECONOMIC GROWTH

"We've inherited one hell of a mess. Layoffs around the country are worse than we thought. Government must create more jobs and better incomes and opportunities for hard-pressed working families." [1]

-Bill Clinton

"Everyone should come to work for the Federal Government," said Bill Clinton on February 3, 1993 in a speech to the employees of the Office of Management and Budget.[2] In 1948, one in ten Americans worked for federal, state and local governments. By 1994, one in seven Americans was a government employee. When one American in three works for government, will tax rates be higher or lower? Will the federal deficit be larger or smaller? When problems arise, do government antidotes tend to increase or decrease the number of government workers? What occurs when general populations increase at 1 to 2 percent average annual rates of growth while bureaucrats increase like rabbits? When everyone works for government, will America run out of problems?

Five thousand years ago, governments constructed towering pyramids in Egypt's valley of the Nile. The work force necessary to execute these monuments was enormous. Unemployment was virtually unknown.

Five thousand years later, President Clinton wants to use government to continue to erect more pyramids which are prized for the economic benefits they seemingly bestow.

We crack the whip to get things done,
our projects make the country run.
Colossal works which rise so tall,
give rise to pride but that's not all.
Jobless woes we Pharaohs rid,
each time we build a pyramid.

Witness however, their impact on Tom, Dick and Harry.

Tom labors on a construction project funded by Congress. Its purpose? To "create jobs for the unemployed." See Tom work.

Dick has just computed his annual tax liability. He owes the IRS eight thousand dollars. Dashed are Dick's plans to remodel his bakery. Gone are Dick's dreams and aspirations. See Dick cry.

And Harry? Harry is the idle carpenter who was never employed by Dick because Dick's bakery profits were requisitioned by the government for "higher purposes." See Harry loaf!

As federally funded pyramids rise from the ground, onlookers admire each emerging configuration, and newspapers write glowing words about all the wonderful benefits. And look, Tom has a job.

But pyramid schemes extract their toll . . .

Unemployment benefits have just been extended for Harry. Another tax increase supporting a new federal jobs bill to employ Tom is pending . . . and seeking a bank loan to "save his buns" is Dick, the tax battered baker.

Increased government spending always means less private spending. Looking behind government jobs, aid, and training, we find thousands of people that could have been hired, thousands of projects that would have been undertaken and thousands of market investments that should have taken place. Jobs, projects, and investments that are lost forever because of the Law of Lemons.

- OBSERVATION -

It seems that much economic misery stems
from the irrevocable Law of Lemons . . .
When some get government aid,
others feel the squeeze!

WORKERS WOULD BENEFIT IF LABOR UNIONS HAD MORE CLOUT

"In order to maintain themselves, unions have got to have some ability to strap their members to the mast." [adding that] "the only way unions can exercise countervailing power vis-à-vis management is to hold their members' feet to the fire when times get tough . . . Otherwise, the organization is only as good as it is convenient for any given member at any given time." [3]

-Robert Reich

There once was a mannequin who fired a mannequin
who wouldn't budge from his fat canakin.

Can a mannequin can* a mannequin?
In our free land, of course, he canakin.

Unless it irks old Uncle Samakin
or a union girl or mannequin

Each of which can ban a canakin.
That's why folks buy
more from Japanakin!

(* can, as in "get fired")

Reich lobbied hard for the Anti-Striker Replacement Act which would prevent firms from hiring replacements for striking workers. Unfortunately, the strike bill comes from a paternalistic mind set holding that unions should be made powerful by granting them coercive power over working people for their own good, whether they like it or not.

The problem is much deeper than replacements. The Department of Labor has released a study to show the next few years are going to be the biggest strike years since Jimmy Carter was president. Walkouts by workers at UPS, Pittsburgh Steel, General Motors and Caterpillar look like the tip of an upcoming iceberg.

Why such unrest?

The main reason is that President Clinton and Secretary of Labor Reich have filled the National Labor Relations Board with pro-union people. Chairman William Gould, a former Stanford professor, has stated he has a "definite pro-union agenda."

So much for the golden era of labor-business cooperation ballyhooed during the last campaign.

The anti-competitive aspects of unions are what really hurt the economy. Locking productive people out while simultaneously locking all union people in is hardly a healthy prescription for economic opportunity and growth.

A new commission established in March, 1993 by Labor Secretary Reich, called the Commission on the Future of Worker-Management Relations, will be Clinton's vehicle for enacting labor law reform demanded by the AFL-CIO. Recommendations will include allowing unions to represent temporary workers as well as managers and supervisors presently without union representation. Employers will be required to: bargain with unions representing *both* a majority and minority of workers; give representation privileges based on employee signatures on union "authorization cards"; and be willing to give up present National Labor Relations Board elections that often give union members the chance to decertify and absolve themselves from union membership.

It will be interesting to watch Clinton and Reich maneuver their plan through a newly elected Republican House and Senate.

A PERSONAL EXAMPLE:

I speak to business people throughout the world. Most of the meetings are held in large hotels. Since each conference room is different and could cause problems, I try to check it out the night before and do my best to make it "audience friendly." In doing so, I usually have to work with unionized technicians, sound people and hotel help.

"Sir," I say to the union worker. "That big light shining from the middle of the ceiling is glaring from the mirrors in the front of the room and will make it very uncomfortable for those in the audience. Could you dim it, please?"

"No," he answers, "all the lights are on the same switch. Do you want the switch on or off?"

"Well, what happens when it's off?" I ask.

"Darkness," he replies.

"Well, could we get a ladder and, perhaps, unscrew the bulb?" I ask.

"No," he answers. "The hotel does not have a fourteen foot ladder, and besides, we would have to bring in an electrician. I am not allowed to mess with things like that."

"Well, could you get an electrician?" I beg.

"No," he retorts. "They are all off work this time of night."

So much for the light.

Then I tell him that I need a wireless microphone.

"A wireless what?" he snorts. I don't think we have one."

"But I'm sure the association ordered one for me. They always do," I reply.

"Listen friend," he says. "My union tells me what I can and cannot do. I don't know if you can find the right guy, but I'll tell you right now that if you do, you'll definitely need an invoice!"

Labor unions? More clout? Give me a break.

MINIMUM WAGE LAWS COMBAT POVERTY

"Reich suggested a massive, guaranteed federal retraining program for anyone poor, unemployed, or on welfare" to show that "Clinton was serious about human capital . . . and FDR-style programs." [4]

-Woodward on Robert Reich

There once was a widow named Cora
who sat with the baby next door-a.
'Till minimum wage
became the great rage
now Cora don't sit there no more-a.

"Ten dollars per hour," cried Cora,
"has made me a great deal more poor-a.
It isn't enjoyable
to be unemployable,
please cut my wage hike, I implore-a."

"Don't worry," said Secretary Reich.
"Dear Cora, I know it's been rough.
If you are unable
to set a full table,
food stamps will buys lots of good stuff."

Minimum wage laws hurt most the very people they are designed to help. Government cannot make a person worth more by making it illegal for anyone to offer them less. We merely deprive them of the right to earn the amount that their abilities and opportunities would allow them to earn. Apparently government believes that no job at $4.65 an hour is better than having a job at $3.00 an hour.

Minimum wage laws allegedly protect marginally skilled workers who might otherwise receive less than adequate compensation. Hence their appeal to large voting blocks and the leaders they elect.

In practice, each minimum wage hike increases the number of unemployed workers!

If Congress enacted a ten-dollar-per-hour minimum wage law and expanded coverage to include the profession of baby-sitting, all but a tiny handful of sitters would be rendered unemployable.

Should we worry about the minimum wage? A few facts.[5]

Most workers earning the minimum wage are not poor, nor are they likely to be stuck in their low-paying job. More than 50 percent of minimum wage workers are between sixteen and twenty-four years old. Eighty percent of all minimum wage employees live in non-poor households and almost 20 percent live in households with annual incomes above fifty thousand dollars. More than 63 percent work only part time.

Evidence shows that the overwhelming majority of employees simply grow out of minimum-wage jobs as their work skills and job experience increase.

Within a year after starting minimum-wage employment, 63 percent of employees still working on an hourly basis are making more than the minimum, with the median increase amounting to nearly 20 percent. Only a very few, mostly those who lack a high school diploma or who work part-time, fail to advance.

Although single parents are frequently mentioned by those calling for a higher minimum wage, fewer than half a million single parents earn the minimum wage. Further, as a result of government formulas that determine the amount of transfer payments, single parents may actually be made worse off if the minimum wage is increased. A single parent, with one child, who works full-time is up to $1,800 worse off as a result of the last increase because the family's public benefits fell (and its taxes rose) by more than the increase in earnings.

In 1981, 15 percent of the hourly work force was paid at or near the minimum wage. By 1992, this figure had fallen to 7.6 percent, and it continues to go down.

LOW INTEREST RATES ARE THE LINCHPIN OF CLINTONOMICS

*"[Deficit reduction] has been the principal factor in the dramatic **decline in long-term interest rates**."*
President Bill Clinton
Economic Report of the President—Feb. 13, 1994

*"Lloyd Bentsen, as the leader of our economic team, has been doing an absolutely superb job in helping the president and Bob Rubin and others, Laura Tyson, get this whole—Leon Panetta—get the whole deficit coming down and **interest rates down** and getting the economy moving again."*
Vice President Al Gore
NBC's "Today Show"—Jan. 20, 1994

*"Since the election, and since the public has realized the president's commitment to deficit reduction, **interest rates have started down**. In fact they have fallen so far that a homeowner with a variable rate loan or who refinanced a higher rate mortgage would already be able to pay the energy tax and have plenty left over."*
Former Treasury Secretary Lloyd Bentsen
Senate Budget Committee—Feb. 18, 1994

*"Our economic program made a recovery possible by **lowering interest rates**, facilitating private investment, and building consumer confidence . . . We think it is really quite simple. A growing economy rests on companies that*

grow. Government must become a productive partner in their growth. We do that with a fiscal policy that lets low interest rates drive investment."

Commerce Secretary Ron Brown
Carnegie Endowment—March 3, 1994

*"The economy is being driven . . . by the interest-sensitive components of spending. These are the areas of the economy that have benefited tremendously by the **historic low interest rates** which have been encouraged by our budget and deficit reduction effort."*

Council of Economic Advisors Chairwoman
Laura D'Andrea Tyson
White House—Dec. 2, 1993

Excuse me . . . ?

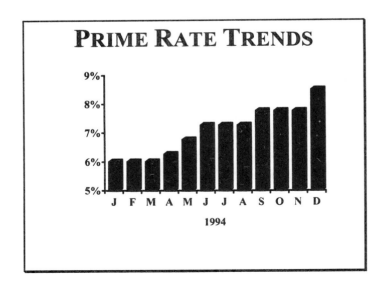

Chapter Thirteen

GOVERNMENT REGULATION
AND SAFETY

"We must provide the answers, the solutions. And we will." [1]

-Bill Clinton

In an economy throttled by "dictocratic benevolence," it becomes increasingly difficult for anyone to get anything off the ground. Do safety benefits bestowed by government outweigh human and economic costs? Has the Occupational Safety and Health Act made America a safer place in which to work? Can workers bank on government as a great protector?

The costs of government regulations on Americans have not been a very high priority issue in recent years. And that is a national tragedy because the price is getting very high.

We really should give credit
to OSHA when it's due.
They came across an airplane
and two members of a crew.

Who had no safety seatbelt
or de-icing on their wings,
and safety checks clearly showed
a thousand other things.

That led to an injunction
against all further flight.
Then heavy fines were levied
as OSHA flexed its might.

Our hats go off to OSHA
for saving life and limb.
Those looney Wrights at Kittyhawk
will never fly again!

- OBSERVATION -

OSHA is better at wronging Wrights,
than righting wrongs.

Federal regulations, which were held at bay during the Reagan years, began growing again under George Bush. The number of new regulations has since taken a giant leap upward under Clinton, who has a government plan for every problem, a subsidy for every need and a regulation for every activity.

While there are many taxpayers who think government doesn't do anything well, they are wrong. When it comes to making regulations, government can compete with anybody.

- OBSERVATION -

If you think OSHA
is a small town in Wisconsin,
have I got news for you.

WHEN CONSUMERS ARE UNABLE TO PROTECT THEMSELVES, PRUDENCE CALLS FOR GOVERNMENT SOLUTIONS

"American workers are not going to be sacrificed at the altar of profits. Unfortunately, some blue-collar workers today fear they have to choose between their job and a safe job." [2]

-Robert Reich

Super liberals like Reich are an interesting breed. They just love employment. But they can't stand employers. They always assume the worst when it comes to private employers, and the best when it comes to political solutions. Reich actually believes the words government and efficiency belong in the same sentence. Is there anything outside government's purview?

Each day millions of Americans innocently expose themselves to dangerous bathtub hazards. Each year, bathtubs injure and maim thousands of victims. Should politicians closely examine the problem? Should they act to regulate bathtub safety? Do people who slosh around in search of government solutions usually end up in hot water?

The year was 1994,
when Reich did empower,
bureaucrats to safetytize
each bathtub floor and shower.

To save our hides
from falls and slides,
a billion bucks they spent.
They studied every bathtub
and every accident.

They computerized all data
on everything they learned.
They processed reams of paper,
no soap was left unturned.

And from it all, each tub and stall
a safety sign did get.
Ingeniously, three words decreed
"Slippery When Wet!"

- OBSERVATION -

In the ivory towers of bureaucracy . . .
the end always justifies the reams!

On Friday, August 12, 1994, Secretary of Labor Reich called Bridgestone/Firestone, Inc., in Oklahoma City to say he was about to charge them with safety violations. An hour later, flanked by local police and Secret Service escorts, the labor secretary marched past a phalanx of television cameras and into the Dayton plant. Mr. Reich's dramatic moves were intended to show the Clinton Administration's determination to re-invigorate the government's far reaching regulatory apparatus after twelve years of Republican rule. [3]

But guess what? Most workers at Bridgestone/Firestone don't agree with the Labor Secretary. He was condescending and paternalistic, many said. With public confidence in government at a historic low and concern about job security very high, efforts by officials such as Mr. Reich run into a barrage of skepticism.

There is a growing disillusionment. "People are swirling around in this maze, uncertain about their own job security. They're paying higher taxes. Then they see the government coming in with all these new regulations and fines. Where is the logic? Where is the sense? They don't see a benefit for themselves," said Deborah Bright, a New York consultant who has counseled a slew of major companies and their employees during the layoffs of recent years.

Indeed, just as Mr. Reich left Oklahoma City, the backlash began. The Dayton Tire plant closed down for a day because, its executives said, they couldn't comply with Mr. Reich's orders. The local newspaper attacked the secretary in an editorial headlined "Reich's Amerika" and ran a cartoon of the diminutive official next to a giant tire captioned: "Time to Retire?"

The Dayton Tire workers didn't rally to the cause. In fact, they proved more suspicious of Mr. Reich than of Dayton Tire. "He came here with his guns cocked and just didn't know what the hell he was doing," says Larry Pierce, a Dayton worker.

To Virginia Jolley, a Dayton Tire worker since 1982, "It was all political. I felt he was trying to further the Clinton Administration. He was just so cocky." And Alex Compton, a 10-year employee at the company, calls the secretary "an outsider" seeking "a showboat for power."

The crowning blow against the Labor Department was delivered the day after Mr. Reich's visit by Federal District Judge Timothy Leonard. The Oklahoma City judge dissolved the emergency order against Dayton Tire; he didn't think the workers faced any imminent danger. Later, he also denied the government's request for a preliminary injunction against the company. The charges are still pending before the Occupational Safety and Health Administration. The case could drag on a year or more.

Many local people say the government was heavy-handed in swooping into town and slapping a company with a huge fine. "Too much power, it sounds like to me," says Rick Chesser, a local farmer who grows wheat and alfalfa on Dayton Tire land. "It's kind of frightening, isn't it?"

Down the road at Western Heights High School, Joe Carter, the girls' basketball coach, says: "We don't think much of these decisions from a person in Washington."

AN ASMUS AXIOM

(D.O.L.) + (E.P.A.) + (H.U.D.) + (H.H.S.) + (D.O.E.) = (M.O.B.)*

*Members of Bureaucracy

- OBSERVATION -

The aggregate of all problems
worked on by all government agencies
is not so great as the problem posed by
the aggregate of all government agencies.

CONSUMER LAWS HELP CONSUMERS

"A Clinton Administration won't spend our money on programs that don't solve problems and a government that doesn't work. I want to reinvent government to make it more efficient and more effective. I want to give citizens more choices in the services they get, and empower them to make those choices." [4]

-Bill Clinton

When Cousin Zeke choked last week
on a cube of ice he swallowed,
consumer groups expressed outrage
and action swiftly followed.

Ice makers all were banned from use
by Federal decrees.
Consumers are protected now
from hardening of the wateries!

- OBSERVATION -

Ask government to protect consumers, and consumers will eventually lose their cool.

The Lord's Prayer contains 66 words, the Gettysburg Address has 286 words, and there are 1,322 words in the Declaration of Independence. Yet, government regulations on the sale of cabbage total 26,911 words.

But just when you may have thought that the regulation binge can't possibly get any worse, the Clinton Administration is showing us that it can, it has, and it will.

Last year's Federal Register, the government's encyclopedia of regulations, was the third largest volume ever. Its 69,688 pages are exceeded only by the last two years of the Carter Administration. And that was only the first year of what Clinton and Gore have planned for us.

All told, government regulations will cost our country an estimated $655 billion this year, or $2,600 per capita. Put that in perspective. Every month you must write out a check to government for $216.66 to pay for regulations mandated in Washington, D.C. Of course, if you are married and have two children, make that check $866 each month.

The Office of Management and Budget estimates that government paperwork forces the business sector to put in five billion more hours per year at a cost of $100 billion. All of this is passed along to consumers in the cost of everything they buy.

Politicians, in the belief that they will be rewarded by anxious voters for doing something, have attempted an impossible task: to idiot-proof society. Regulations and mandates imposed on all for the sake of a very few are very costly. Tragically, our liberties are trampled in the rush to eradicate risk.

Chapter   Fourteen

THE ENVIRONMENT

"Our insatiable drive to rummage deep beneath the surface of the earth, remove all the coal, petroleum, and other fossil fuels we can find, then burn them as quickly as they are found—in the process filling the atmosphere with carbon dioxide and other pollutants—is a willful expansion of our dysfunctional civilization into vulnerable parts of the natural world." [1]

-Al Gore

My, my, Mr. Vice President. And I thought the point of all that fossil fuel was to heat our homes and run our cars. With views like yours OUR DAYS ARE NUMBERED.

IN THE BEGINNING vehicles of locomotion were prevalent on the face of the land, and beneath its surface, man the producer, extracted a substance from which the locomotion derived its sustenance. But, there were saviors of the earth who saw evil in that which oozed dark and murky—so they prayed for the spirit of government to restore the primeval state which existed prior to the age of locomotion.

AND SO IT CAME TO PASS:

ON THE FIRST DAY government said unto man "Thou shalt not search the shallow waters for the source of locomotion!" Thus, dominion was restored to the creatures that swimmeth, and government said "this was good."

ON THE SECOND DAY government again spoke unto man saying, "Thou shalt not desecrate the surface of the land." Thus, man the producer was forever banished from the wilderness, and government said "this was good."

ON THE THIRD DAY government caused a flood of environmental commandments to inundate the land. Man the producer became ensnarled by the deluge and the commandments prevailed and even increased until there were ten thousand commandments. Beneath the torrent, production perished and government said "this was good."

ON THE FOURTH DAY locomotion faltered and anguish swept the land. Guilt was cast at man the producer and man the merchant and man the voracious consumer. Gore said "this was *very* good."

ON THE FIFTH DAY a swarm of bureaucrats descended upon the multitudes, commanding them to share that which remained of the dark substance. Thus, sharing was instilled in the heart of man and government saw the equality of it all and government said "this was good."

ON THE SIXTH DAY government finished its work, yet the sorrows of man multiplied. That which was no longer extracted no longer existed, thus sharing ceased. Beasts of burden replaced the vehicles of locomotion and man reigned as the supreme beast. Worry lined his forehead. Sweat flooded his brow. Misery accompanied him throughout all the years of his life. Thus, nature replaced the age of locomotion. . .

AND THERE WOULD BE NO DAY OF REST!

There is a better way. What if Gore would consider the following common-sense approach?

To insure cleaner air: reduce auto emissions by using congestion fees and fines, give plant owners and managers flexibility to meet emission goals, and allow tradable emission permit systems. Then, go back to the tried and true common law remedies to air pollution. And finally: do not put caps or carbon taxes on carbon dioxide emissions. The cost is overwhelming compared to the benefits.

Market economists would agree that the single biggest environmental policy failure of the past twenty years has been the mistake of imposing mandates instead of providing incentives for the private sector to improve the environment. Robert Hohn, an adjunct research fellow at Harvard University, has estimated that consumers will pay between $8 billion and $22 billion more for pollution control with vehicle mandates in the Northeast and California than they would if less expensive pollution control technologies were used. Under a market-based approach, he says, government would set the upper limit on emissions and then leave it up to business managers as to how best meet the requirement. The answer of replacing mandates with markets would literally save billions of dollars and unleash technological innovation that would lead to more rapid environmental progress.[2]

Market solutions abound, Mr. Vice President. How about taking a look?

"WE ARE BULLDOZING THE GARDEN OF EDEN"

"Our inability to provide adequate protection for the world's food supply is, in my opinion, simply another manifestation of the same philosophical error that has led to the global environmental crisis as a whole: we have assumed that our lives need have no real connection to the natural world, that our minds are separate from our bodies, and that as disembodied intellects we can manipulate the world any way we choose." [3]

-Al Gore

―――――――――

Farmer John! Shame on you.
In all that soil you dig into
we found some dirt and when it blows
the dust you raise clogs the nose.

So, park your tractors, you won't miss 'em.
Stop treading on our ecosystem!

And do it now—your dust is treason.
We demand a sneeze free season.

At EPA, because we care,
folks are starving to breathe clean air.

―――――――――

- OBSERVATION -

If the Environmental Protection Agency
ever rids the air of contaminants,
acclaim will be short lived.

If you read *Time, Newsweek,* or Al Gore's book, and
watch television programs such as "Phil Donahue" or the
network evening news, you have been told repeatedly that
our world is getting dirtier, not cleaner.

If these accounts are true, then surely life today is less
safe and less healthy than it was a generation ago. If we
are bulldozing the Garden of Eden, and Gore is right,
widespread concern over air and water pollution, solid
waste disposal, and natural resource depletion would seem
to be justified.

But, there is one little problem with these stories. They
are false. Dr. Elizabeth Whelan, executive director of the
American Council on Science and Health, author of
twelve books on health issues, and a graduate of the
Harvard School of Public Health and the Yale School of
Medicine, writes:

> I have reviewed literally thousands of popular and scientific
> articles on the topic of environmental factors and human
> health. . . . What I found in my literature review was an
> astounding gap between the consensus in the scientific and
> medical community on environmental issues, versus what is
> being presented in popular publications, on television and
> radio, and in books for the layman. [4]

At the 1992 Earth Summit in Rio de Janeiro, a group of 425 scientists and economists, including 27 Nobel laureates, decried the inaccuracy and exaggeration that has come to characterize the positions of leading environmental organizations. Twenty-seven hundred scientists, professors, and other intellectual leaders signed this rebuttal[5]:

> We are . . . worried, at the dawn of the 21st Century, at the emergence of an irrational ideology that is opposed to scientific and industrial progress and impedes economic and social development . . . We intend to assert science's responsibility and duties toward society as a whole. We do, however, forewarn the authorities in charge of our planet's destiny against decisions which are supported by pseudoscientific arguments or false and irrelevant data. . . . The greatest evils which stalk our earth are ignorance and oppression, not science, technology, and industry.

The views of the alarmists have been proven to be wrong. Most trends—cancer rates, air and water quality, human health, wooded land acreage, and a dozen other indicators of environmental quality in the U.S.—show improvement, not decline. Global trends also show improvement, though less dramatically than trends in the U.S. Although generalizations are difficult to make in the complex arena of environmental quality, available evidence supports the following observation: Most Americans today live in an environment that is safer than it was at any time in the past half-century.

TO IMPROVE MAN'S QUALITY OF LIFE ON EARTH, MAN MUST LEARN TO ADAPT TO NATURE

"Global warming, ozone depletion, the loss of living species, deforestation—they all have a common cause: the new relationship between human civilization and the earth's natural balance" [6]

-Al Gore

What is likely to kill off the human race first? Global warming? The ozone depletion? Over population? Chemicals and insecticides? The answer? None of these. Apocalypse prophets mislead and scare, but they don't inform. Gore reminds me of the patient of Carl Jung who lived in constant fear of cancer. Jung wrote: "I recall a professor of philosophy who once consulted me about his cancer phobia. He suffered from a compulsive conviction that he had a malignant tumor, although nothing of the kind was ever found in dozens of x-ray pictures. 'Oh, I know there is nothing,' he would say, 'but there *might* be something.'"

Tragically linked to these apocalypse myths are unintended consequences such as reduced life expectancies, restricted food production, and lower living standards, especially for the poor. Such consequences must be included in future discussions concerning the quality of life on this planet.

Where nature rules
no man has died
from poisoned air
or pesticide.

Where nature rules
the clear blue skies
harbor swarms
of Tsetse flies.

Where nature rules
swarms of Tsetse
have earmarked man
endangered species.

Where nature rules
the air is clean
but few survive
past sweet sixteen.

Where nature rules
the fair conclusion
is—they could use
some air pollution!

- OBSERVATION -

The back-to-nature movement is full of bugs!

Environmentalists see nature as serene and benign, a gorgeous painting of snow-capped peaks, of mountain ranges, plateaus, meadows, lakes, and streams . . . retreats for the mystically inclined, and ever-productive—when man doesn't interfere—of natural, healthful, organic foods untouched by poisonous, death-dealing chemical insecticides. Not often are we reminded that nature is also a composite of terrifying, atmosphere polluting volcanoes, of devastating earthquakes, hurricanes and tidal waves, of droughts and floods, of lethal insects, snakes, and wild animals, and of literally trillions upon trillions of microscopic organisms waiting, it may fairly be said, for man's technological guard to drop in order to commence their onslaughts against health and life. Man's greatest accomplishment on earth is the development of cities and thus civilization, and this development has always been and must be at the expense of the environmentalists beloved wilderness, a form of love that only an advanced technology and an upper-class mode of living makes attractive.

-Robert Nisbet

Nature was raw and cruel to nature long before human beings intervened. It may be doubted whether human beings have ever done one-tenth of the polluting to nature that nature has done to itself. There is infinitely more methane gas—poisonous in one respect, and damaging to the environment—generated by the swamps of Florida and other parts of the United States than by all the automobile pollution of all the places on this planet. In our super-human efforts to be nice and feel guilty, we sometimes try to take all the credit for pollution improperly.

-Michael Novak

One of the Clinton Administration's goals is to move farmers toward natural, non-chemical methods to control pests—for example, using one species of plant, insect or fungus to kill other undesirable species. Although this goal is politically popular, its feasibility is limited. The natural alternatives available to today's farmer are very limited. What would happen if U.S. farmers substituted currently available non-chemical methods of pest control?

Soybean production would decrease by 37 percent, wheat by 24 percent and cotton by 39 percent. Rice production would decrease by 57 percent, peanuts by 78 percent and field corn by 32 percent. [7]

Natural control methods for many pests, such as the boll weevil, have been researched for a century with very limited success. Further, few non-chemical alternatives fully replace synthetic chemicals.

Natural methods of pest control are generally targeted at a single species, while the chemical pesticides they seek to replace are usually targeted at more than one pest in the same crop.

Thus, scientists may have to develop hundreds of different kinds of natural weed-killers, each effective on a single weed species, to replace one chemical herbicide that controls hundreds of different kinds of weeds.

Some of the natural alternatives may themselves carry unrecognized risks. Insects or natural diseases introduced to control a plant pest may become pests themselves.

AUTOMOBILES ARE DESTROYING OUR ENVIRONMENT

"We now know that the automobile's cumulative impact on the global environment is posing a mortal threat to the security of every nation that is more deadly than that of any military enemy we are ever again likely to confront" [8]

-Al Gore

Wow! Is the Vice President an alarmist, or what? Yes, cars are a highly visible source of pollution. And yes, they do use lots of oil and gasoline. But they are also the way millions of us make our way to jobs, schools, and vacation destinations. Are they really more deadly than that of any military enemy we are every again likely to confront? Or, is it time for Eco-Sanity?

This summer, my family and I spent five glorious days on Macinac Island in upstate Michigan. They do not allow cars on the island; all transportation is by horse and carriage. A few facts: a horse produces approximately 45 pounds of manure each day. The massive accumulations of manure are a never-ending disposal problem. Flies, dried manure, and the odor of urine often fill the air. But imagine what it would be like in a big city! Occupational diseases are still prevalent where horses are used exclusively.

Cars do create pollution. But it's also true that cars have dramatically decreased overall pollution. What about the considerable progress that already has been made in reducing the rate at which individual cars produce pollution? It is one of the most dramatic and unsung environmental success stories of the 1980s and 1990s. Consider the progress:

> Today's new cars emit 97 percent less hydro-carbons, 96 percent less carbon monoxide, and 90 percent less nitrogen oxide than those built twenty years ago.

> Cars purchased in the 1990s will emit about 80 percent less hydrocarbons and 60 percent less nitrogen oxide during their lifetimes, even though they will be owned longer and driven farther.

> Between 1970 and 1991, total highway vehicle emissions of hydra-carbons dropped 66 percent, carbon monoxide emissions by 59 percent, and nitrogen oxide emissions by 21 percent—despite the doubling of vehicle miles traveled. [9]

All of this, however, will soon be a moot point. Within a decade or two, we will all be driving electric cars charged photovoltaically. Renewable energy from the five million quads of energy the sun bountifully pours on earth each year will significantly reduce the pollution levels now produced by our present all-fossil fuel economy.

The E.P.A. should change its name
So truth is plain to see.

They're resurrecting jungle life.
Let's call 'em . . . A.P.E.

Chapter Fifteen

FOOL US ONCE...

"I will put aside my 1996 re-election worries. My rule for the next two years will be country first and politics-as-usual dead last."
-Bill Clinton
Presidential Address
December 15, 1994

═══════════

If tailors restitch their mistakes
and architects plant shrubs,
what does Bill Clinton do
to camouflage his flubs?

In '92, all of you
said change was what was needed.
So he changed and changed until the time
his re-election had succeeded.

═══════════

Bob Woodward's book *The Agenda: Inside the Clinton White House* makes it quite clear that *all* this administration thinks about is politics and re-election. For example:

Clinton's White House, Gergen felt, was surprisingly explicit in discussing matters that had been tucked away in the Republican administrations where he had worked. Clinton and his staff thought and talked a lot about the 1996 reelection effort. A campaign mentality permeated the White House, a War Room mentality (p. 320).

The administration, Stephanopoulos felt, had to find a way of measuring a successful presidency. He realized it all came down to one thing: winning reelection. Clinton had to win again in 1996. Successful presidents were reelected; failed presidents were not. Ronald Reagan, perhaps the worst modern president in Stephanopoulos's view, was widely considered successful, because, he believed, Reagan had won reelection (pp. 329-330).

"You don't understand," Hillary replied. "If we don't get this [health care] done this year, we are three years away from the benefits. And the only savings will be in the fourth year. So we've got to get it done right away, or we're going to be beaten in 1996" (p. 120).

Clinton realized he wasn't the only one who was operating as if the 1996 presidential campaign began the day he became president (p. 105).

How will Clinton reinvent himself? As a man of fixed and unbending principles, his first one is to be flexible at all times. He will propose middle class tax cuts, crime measures and headline-making ways to streamline the federal government. He will fire members of his cabinet, eliminate departments, and overhaul his White House staff. Hillary will be asked to take a lower profile and Vice President Gore will be seen behind, rather than next to the President. Robert Reich, Ira Magaziner, Donna Shalala and other extremely liberal members of his administration will either be replaced or be asked to tone down.

He will try to reinforce his image as a "different kind of Democrat," running away from the tax and spend big government types, and be seen as one who listens to the working and middle class voter.

Will he succeed?

Political analyst Kevin Phillips has written that off-year election landslides—1946, 1958, 1966, and 1974—invariably are followed by very close presidential elections. If history repeats itself, nobody's odds in 1996 are any better than William Jefferson Clinton's, says the *Wall Street Journal*'s liberal, Albert R. Hunt.

Philosophical turn-arounds have happened before. Governor Jerry Brown of California campaigned hard against the Proposition 13 initiative to limit taxes. The night before the election, he was seen on television predicting the demise of California if the Proposition passed. But a funny thing happened. It did. The parade was marching north. Brown was going south. The night of the election, he put on his sneakers, shifted positions, and by the next morning, guess who was leading the Proposition 13 parade?

Clinton will imitate Brown. He got the 1994 election message. He will probably support term limits, a line-item veto, and a balanced budget amendment. He might even lead the anti-government, pro-individual initiative by overthrowing our convoluted tax system and endorsing the flat tax. He will begin to dismantle the welfare state by supporting block grants to the states which will shift responsibility of welfare, food stamps, and other related programs from the federal government.

Health Care policy, however is another question. In 1992 and 1993, the President and his wife argued it was the biggest crisis facing America. Yet, they have been strangely quiet these past two years. I wonder why? Did they misdiagnose the cause? Is government the solution or is government the problem?

Bill Clinton's spent his first three years in a "funk." Will he start over? In golf, it's called a mulligan. If you don't like the shot you hit, drop another ball and hit again. And again. His golfing buddies call him the Master of the Mulligan, taking dozens of second shots, and lengthening the time it takes him to play a round by at least an hour. Americans have noticed a similar pattern with his policies—Welfare, Medicare, and Social Security reform, Bosnia, Haiti, North Korea, gays in the military, educational vouchers, Supreme Court nominations, cabinet appointees, tax cuts, and term limits.

How many mulligans does this guy get?

- OBSERVATIONS -

Challengers beware: Clinton always plays his best
on the back nine.

Clinton beware: Those not rooted in principle
are easily up-rooted.

A Tribute to America

Ladies and Gentlemen, my name is the United States of America. I was born on July 4, 1776, conceived in freedom and liberty. Millions of people have come to my shores to cast their economic plight with me. But that freedom has not been cheap. Hundreds of thousands of my sons and daughters have lost their lives on the battlefields of Europe, Asia and the Persian Gulf. Thousands of families have cried in anguish as they learned their fathers, husbands, sons and daughters were killed in the fight for freedom. But thank God, those lives stood for something.

I am big. From the Atlantic to the Pacific; from the northern reaches of Alaska to the beautiful Hawaiian Islands, I have three and one-half million square miles pulsating with economic activity and opportunity. I have forests in Oregon, wheat fields in Kansas, oil in Texas and coal in Virginia. I am the Empire State Building in New York, the Sears Tower in Chicago, and Disneyland in California.

I have over two million farms whose productivity is unequaled anywhere in the world. I have given birth to thousands, nay millions, of producers and entrepreneurs. Men and women like Cyrus McCormick, Thomas Edison and Henry Ford; up to the contemporaries: Jonas Salk, Stanford and Iris Ovshinsky, Mary Kay Ash—people who have literally changed the face of this country and this world for the better. I am Babe Ruth and the World Series, Vince Lombardi and professional football, Chris Everett and professional tennis. And in my opinion, no one slams it better than Michael "Air" Jordan.

But more than a nation that just works and plays, I am a nation that prays. I have over 450,000 churches and synagogues where people worship the God who is there because He is not silent.

Over two hundred years ago, Thomas Jefferson penned a Declaration that still stands as a beacon for America:

> We hold these truths to be self-evident, that all men are created equal, that they are endowed by their Creator with certain unalienable Rights, that among these are Life, Liberty, and the pursuit of Happiness.

A hundred years later, during the dark hours of the Civil War, Abraham Lincoln was asked the question, "Can a nation of the people, by the people, and for the people survive?" Hesitating for a moment, he replied: "I do not know how history will speak on America. But I do know that Americans were born to be free." [1]

ABOUT THE AUTHOR

Dr. Barry Asmus speaks, writes, and consults on political and business issues facing America. Recognized for his views on making the U.S. a world-class competitor using market incentives, he was twice voted the Outstanding Professor of the Year, as well as receiving the Freedom Foundation at Valley Forge Award for Private Enterprise Education. His weekly commentary can be heard in Los Angeles on radio station KMNY business talk. Dr. Asmus's books include: *Supermyths: An Almanac of Political Fables* (1980) co-author Jerry Hill; *Crossroads: The Great American Experiment* (1984) co-author Don Billings; *The Space Place* (1988); *ClintonCare: Putting Government in Charge of Your Health* (1994); and *It's Tea Time, Again: The Original American Dream* (1995), also co-authored with Dr. Billings. In addition, Asmus is a Senior Economist with the National Center for Policy Analysis. The NCPA provides policy makers with timely, detailed, and accurate information about the impact of proposed policies and legislation. The Center's goal is to promote private alternatives to government regulation and control by relying on the strengths of the competitive, entrepreneurial private sector.

A BRIEF AUTOBIOGRAPHY

I was born and raised on a farm. Some of you had the same experience. You know, there is something about milking cows both morning and night, sitting on a little

Ford tractor cultivating sugar beets and corn 12 hours a day, and standing in cold irrigation water with hip-waders until your bones are about frozen that helps you decide what you don't want to do when you grow up.

"Dad, I don't want to be a farmer."

Now I know that broke his heart. Grandpa had come from Russia and become a farmer. My dad was a farmer. Why couldn't his oldest son be a farmer? Or at the very least, be involved in his tractor and implement business.

"What do you want to do son?" he asked.

"Dad, I want to move into town and someday own and operate a Phillips 66 gas station. Pump gas. Change mufflers. Wash windshields, " I replied. That sounded so much better than farming.

After graduating from high school my dad put his arms around me and said, "Son, Mom and I would be so proud if you went to college."

"College," I said. "But Dad, we've never talked about it."

"I know, son." Dad replied. "But why don't you give it a try."

So off to Colorado State University I went. The first week there I joined a fraternity. I'll never forget sitting on the roof of the ATΩ house, wearing my first pair of Bermuda shorts, surrounded by kegs of beer, and watching more pretty girls go by in an hour than I had seen in my entire life.

The phone rang. It was Dad. "Son, how do you like college?"

"Dad, I just love it," I answered.

Now mind you, I had not even been to one class yet.

In fact, I liked it so well that I got my Bachelors degree, then my Masters, and finally a Ph.D. in economics. It took 10 years.

My Dad at graduation said, "Son, if I would have known you were going to be in college 10 years—why by now we could have owned Phillips 66!"

COMMUNICATING EFFECTIVELY

As an economist, I have the privilege of doing lots of public speaking. Most of the time you need a good story to get the presentation going. I especially enjoy the following one.

It's the story of Albert Einstein dying, going to heaven and St. Peter meeting him at the gate. Unfortunately, the Einstein mansion was not quite completed and St. Peter told him that he would have to live with three roommates for a couple of months.

The first roommate introduced himself by saying that he had an IQ of 180. Einstein returned the greeting by assuring the fellow they would have a great time talking about the theory of relativity.

The second roommate was quick to boast that he had an IQ of 120. Einstein replied, "Terrific, we can discuss the quantum theory of mechanics and examine some mathematical equations."

The third roommate sheepishly made his way up to Einstein and told him his IQ was only 80.

Einstein paused, gave him a long look and asked, "Where do you think interest rates will be going this year?"

Do you want people to listen? Then set the hook with a story. Word pictures are the most powerful form of communication we have. And, if you really want them to listen and remember, use humor. When they're laughing, they're listening.

Of course, humor can be a two-edged sword. Used incorrectly, it can bomb.

For me it happened at Harvard.

It was June 15, 1985. Thirty presidents of the largest banks in the world were having lunch at the home of Harvard's President. I was invited to be the luncheon speaker.

How do you use humor that connects with people from Japan, Australia, France, Spain, Britain, Switzerland, and the U.S.?

I tried. But it was a crackup. Bank presidents are not known for slapping their legs and laughing anyway. The few times I attempted humor—silence. I mean quiet.

See if you can tell what went wrong.

Since they all knew about General Dwight D. Eisenhower, I thought I'd open by telling a funny story about Kruschev and President Eisenhower meeting on Kruschev's visit to the U.S. in 1957.

"How did you do it? How did you do it?" asked Kruschev.

"Do what?" replied Eisenhower.

"My flight was 4 hours late. As we flew in over New York and then down to Washington, I must have seen a million cars on the road."

Eisenhower replied, "So?"

Kruschev asked, "How could you have kept all those cars running for all those hours?"

He truly believed that Eisenhower had brought all the cars in the U.S. to drive on the roads of the New York-Washington, D.C. corridor to impress him.

Eisenhower explained that our highways were always filled with cars.

Kruschev replied with a word. Eisenhower asked, "What did he say?" The interpreter blushed and said sheepishly, "Bull _ _ _ _."

The bankers did not laugh.

I should not have used a swear word, even though it was a quote. And the Presidents of the two largest banks in Tokyo did not appreciate a story about General Eisenhower, even though he commanded the European War and not the Pacific one.

I learned a lot that day.

Know your audience. Who are they? What do they do? What is their job? What are their concerns? What might be most helpful to them? The job is to get in their shoes. I should have spent days researching, telephoning, and making sure I knew something about their banks and particular concerns. The minute people get that look in their eye that says "I don't know what this presentation has to do with me," you know you are in deep trouble.

Unfortunately for me, the only laugh I got that day was mine. Driving from Logan Airport to the college and getting lost near the campus, I stopped to ask a young person crossing the street how to get to Harvard. "Straight A's," he answered.

In retrospect, I should have used that story as my opener.

I try never to forget that the speech I am about to give prospers in direct proportion to the way my audience feels about me. Will they enjoy it? Will they laugh? Is there something special about this presentation? Will they act upon it? Will it really make a difference? Will they feel it? And, if I am invited back, will they feel it again?

Certainly I do not do anything that an audience cannot live without. After all, there are thousands of people who give speeches. Some are good. But very few are exceptional. Exceptional is not a one-shot event, time or place. It is a process which starts with knowing your audience, then delivering with content, enthusiasm, and humor.

I do everything I can to be ready physically. I run three times a week, watch what I eat, and try to get enough sleep. I constantly work on content. Minutes before each speech I go through a special routine. This is it. Go for it. I mean, hit the ball out of the park. Audiences decide whether they are going to like a speech in the first two minutes. It's now or never. You do not get a second chance to make a first impression. Audiences instinctively scan the speaker for sincerity, for character, and for temperament. They can tell whether you are delighted to be there. And, in a very few minutes they decide whether you know what you are talking about.

Light yourself with the fire of enthusiasm, and people will stand in the aisles to watch you burn, says a sign above my desk.

I believe it.

"Nothing great was every achieved without enthusiasm," said Ralph Waldo Emerson.

"There are some who possess the magic touch. It is the infectious spirit of enthusiasm; who have the same effect as a beautiful morning which never reaches noon. Under this spell one's mind is braced, one's spirit recreated; one is ready for any adventure, even if it only be the doing of the next disagreeable task light heartedly," writes Kate Wiggins.

It is relatively easy to give a good talk. But when a speaker visibly enjoys the beliefs they want us to consider, gets excited about the power to change the face of things, and sees in every individual the capacity for significant achievement, exceptionalism is born.

Light yourself with the fire of enthusiasm, and people will stand in the aisles to watch you burn.

In the final analysis, the speech that really matters is the speech that challenges both the heart and the mind. It is an experience which telescopically lengthens one's vision and clarifies one's uncertainty. It is a presentation that provides a mountain-top from which one can gain a wider perspective; an example that can strengthen the appetite for excellence; and, ultimately, encourages each individual toward achievement, responsibility, a better life, and a smile.

In every speech I give I realize that today is my future. There are no excuses. Even a small audience of bankers from a dozen different countries can be entertained and challenged. But, it isn't easy. As J. P. Getty said, the key to success is: (1) get up early, (2) work hard, and (3) discover oil. For most speakers, the oil is content and countenance. Read, read, read. Then smile, and have fun.

Recently, I had to learn that lesson again.

When the Clinton health care plan was released mid-1993, I was very concerned. It was the most massive entitlement ever proposed and would put government, rather than patients, in charge of people's health.

The 1,341 page Clinton Health Security Act used the words "require" 901 times; "limit" 231 times; "penalty" 111 times; "enforce" 83 times; "prohibit" 47 times; "restrict" 35 times; "sanction" 21 times; "prison" 7 times; "fine" 6 times and "ban" once. In fact, the words penalty, restrict, and violate appear more times in President Clinton's health care bill than in his crime bill.

Regional health alliances, community ratings, and managed competition could only mean one thing. Government was about to take over 1/7th of the U.S. economy.

Now, what does one do?

My first approach was to grit my teeth and let the Clintons have it.

"We know what socialism looks like," I said. "Red Square, the Berlin Wall, Castro's Cuba, the Kremlin. But what does socialism sound like?"

"Listen to the sounds of the Clinton Health Care plan—National Health Board, Gatekeepers, Price Controls—does that sound like socialism to you? "

Those are strong words.

Everyone knows that the Clintons mean well and that they really do care about us and our health. Unfortunately, their policy would destroy the greatest health care system in the world. Sometimes, good intentions are not good enough. But, using the word socialism was too inflammatory.

So, what do you think happened the next time out when I laughed, enjoyed myself and tried the following words?

"The President says that the problem with health care is that it is costly, inefficient, and has too much paperwork. So, what is his solution to the problem of cost, inefficiency and paperwork?

Government! I'm not kidding. Government.

Do you really believe the words government and efficiency belong in the same sentence?

Go ahead. Say it. Government cost control. Say it again.

You have just uttered the ultimate oxymoron. It's like saying jumbo shrimp, or Postal Service, or Rapid City, South Dakota.

Consider this: the President has put an attorney in charge of making doctors cheaper!

You could give the government the Sahara and in five years there would be a shortage of sand."

Well guess what? People laughed. And they listened.

I think it entirely proper to take ideas seriously. But never, never take yourself too seriously. Especially if you are an economist.

A man writes to Dear Abby. He says, "I have two brothers and two sisters. My one brother is an economist. My other brother is in prison for committing murder and my two sisters are in prison for burglary. My mother was committed to a mental institution when I was a young boy and my dad has never been able to support the family because of a gambling habit. Abby, I have fallen in love with this beautiful girl. We are going to get married. Abby, here is my question: Should I tell her about my economist brother?"

People who have introduced me have told every economist joke known.

An economist is a person who talks about things you don't understand and makes you believe it's your own fault; a fortune teller with a job.

An economist is a man who would marry Farrah Fawcett for her money.

With most economists, good news is not news.

Most of us chose to become economists because we did not have the personality to become an accountant.

December and January are the months that many economists are called upon to provide economic forecasts for the coming year. That too provides an opportunity for fun.

Forecasting is very difficult, especially if it's about the future.

Those who live by the crystal ball soon learn to eat cracked glass.

The moment you forecast you know you're going to be wrong. You just don't know when and in which direction.

Economists state their GDP growth projections to the nearest tenth of a percentage point to prove they have a sense of humor.

Economic forecasting is the occupation that gives astrology respectability.

The groundhog is like most economists; it delivers its prediction and then disappears.

Give them a number or give them a date, but never both.

When asked to explain your forecast, never underestimate the power of a platitude.

Economists have predicted eight of the last three recessions.

Lastly, and a reminder from my father: An economist's guess is liable to be just as good as anybody else's.

Well, Dad. I gave it my best shot.

It's now time for the market to speak.

ACKNOWLEDGMENTS

Writing a book is not a solo experience. I am grateful for the wisdom of the many speakers, writers, and friends who have influenced its outcome.

There are a few people, however, who deserve special mention for their words and books. In alphabetical order, they are:

Bill Buckley, Don Billings, Darryl DelHousaye, Peter Drucker, Pete duPont, Steve Forbes, Milton Friedman, George Gilder, John Goodman, Jerry Hill, Dwight Lee, Richard McKenzie, John Naisbitt, Tom Peters, Robert Poole, Michael Rothschild, Meg Wheatley, Bob Woodward, and Walter Wriston.

I also want to thank David Henderson, Mark Holmlund, Mike Slominski, and Gayle Tofani for reading the entire manuscript and making helpful suggestions.

Last, I want to thank my wife, Mandy. She would agree that it is quite an experience to live with someone who speaks and travels for a living. Without her support and encouragement, this book would not have happened. Thank you, sweetheart. You make coming home the highlight of my day.

NOTES

Chapter Five
[1]Tom Peters, "A Paean to Self-Organization," *Forbes ASAP*, 10 Oct. 1994: p. 154-56.

Chapter Seven
[1]Walter Williams, "Sagging at the SAT's," *Washington Times*, 1 Jan. 1991: p. 11.
[2]John H. Bishop, "Is the Test Score Decline Responsible for the Productivity Growth Decline?" *American Economic Review*, vol. 79, no. 1 March 1989: pp. 178-97.
[3]David Henderson, "The Case for School Choice," *Hoover Institution, Essays in Public Policy*, no. 44: p. 28

Chapter Eight
[1]Barry Goldwater, *The Conscience of a Conservative* (Washington, D.C.: Regnery Gateway, 1990) p. 17.

Chapter Nine
[1]Bill Clinton and Al Gore, *Putting People First: How We Can All Change America* (Times Books: New York, 1992) p. 222.
[2]Floyd G. Brown, *Slick Wille: Why America Cannot Trust Bill Clinton* (Annapolis: Annapolis-Washington Book Publishers, Inc., 1992) p. 63.
[3]Robert Reich and Ira Magaziner, *Minding America's Business: The Decline and Rise of the American Economy* (New York: Harcourt, 1982) p. 202.

Chapter Ten
[1]Clinton and Gore 107.
[2]*Washington Post*, July 12, 1993; quoted in "To Be Governed," *Policy Report*, September/October 1993.
[3]Woodward 200.
[4]Michael Duffy and Dick Thompson, "I'm Having Nightmares," *Time* 24 May 1993: p. 38.
[5]Many of the statistics in this section came from David R. Henderson, senior research fellow at the Hoover Institution, and editor of *The Fortune Encyclopedia of Economics*. He served as senior health economist with President Reagan's Council of Economic Advisors.

[6]Pat Rooney of Golden Rule Insurance Company in Indianapolis, Indiana is providing companies with the information they need to establish Medical Savings Account programs. If you want information on Medical Savings Accounts for your company, please call 1-800-444-8990.

Chapter Eleven
[1]Clinton and Gore 191.
[2]Richard Vedder and Lowell Gallaway, "The War on the Poor," *IPI Policy Report* No. 177, June 1992.
[3]Woodward 132.
[4]Woodward 26.
[5]Woodward 116.
[6]Woodward 302.
[7]Aldona Robbins and Gary Robbins, "Tax Fairness: Myths and Realitites," *National Center for Policy Analysis Policy Report*, No. 156

Chapter Twelve
[1]Woodward 112.
[2]Woodward 115.
[3]"Jobs: Skills Before Credentials," Wall Street Journal, 2 Feb. 1994: A36
[4]Woodward 36.
[5]"The Minimum Wage: Good Social Policy?" *Employment Policies Institute, Executive Alert*, July/Aug. 1993: p. 1.

Chapter Thirteen
[1]Clinton and Gore 196.
[2]Asra W. Nomani, "Muffed Mission: Labor Secretary's Bid to Push Plant Safety Turns into Skepticism," *Wall Street Journal*, 19 Aug. 1994: p. 1
[3]"Muffed Mission" 1.
[4]Clinton and Gore 196.

Chapter Fourteen
[1]Al Gore, *Earth in the Balance: Ecology and the Human Spirit* (New York: Houghton Mifflin, 1992) p. 234.
[2]Robert Hohn, "Let Markets Drive Down Auto Emissions," *Wall Street Journal*, 17 Oct. 1994: p. A14.
[3]Gore 144.
[4]Joseph L Bast, Peter J. Hill, and Richard C. Rue, Eco-Sanity: A Common-Sense Guide to Environmentalism (Lanham: Madison Books, 1994) p. 8.
[5]Bast, Hill, and Rue 9.
[6]Gore 31.

[7]Leonard Gianessi, "The Quixotic Quest for Chemical-Free Farming," Issues in Science and Technology, Fall 1993, Vol 10, No. 1: p. 11.
[8]Gore 325.
[9]Bast, Hill, and Rue 111.

A Tribute to America
[1]I wrote this tribute to celebrate the re-dedication of the Statue of Liberty in 1986. My German-Russian grandparents came to Ellis Island early this century as did millions of other immigrants. This tribute is to them and to all who have achieved the American dream.

INDEX